Arbitrage

Arbitrage

Opportunities and techniques in the financial and commodity markets

Edited by Rudi Weisweiller

A Wiley Publication

John Wiley & Sons
New York

Published in the USA by John Wiley & Sons, Inc., New York

First published 1986

© Rudi Weisweiller 1986

ISBN 0-471-85382-8

Library of Congress Catalog Card No. 86-15931

Conditions of sale
All rights reserved. No part of this publication may be reproduced, stored in a retrieval system or transmitted, in any form or by any means, electronic, mechanical, photocopying, recording or otherwise, without the prior permission of the copyright owner.

Library of Congress Cataloging in Publication Data
Arbitrage: opportunities and techniques in the
　financial and commodity markets.

　1. Arbitrage.　　I. Weisweiller, Rudi.
HG6024.A3A73　　1986　　332.64′5　　86-15931
ISBN 0-471-85382-8

Printed in Great Britain

Contents

	The contributors	ix
	Editor's preface	xi
1	**What is arbitrage?**	1
	Rudi Weisweiller	
2	**Interest arbitrage**	10
	Ernest Angell	
	The underlying concept	10
	Uncovered interest arbitrage	11
	Interest rate comparisons	12
	Uncovered exchange risks	12
	Possible acceptance of exchange risk	14
	Longer term exchange risk	14
	Problems of exchange risk acceptance	15
	Fully covered interest arbitrage	16
	Compounding	20
	Open positions	22
	Swapping	23
	Management: control and accounting	25
	Internal deals	27
	Conclusion	29
3	**Securities arbitrage**	32
	Mungo Henderson and Ray Martine	
	Historical background	32
	Primary markets	34
	Classical arbitrage: an example	35
	Opportunity creation	35
	Currency conversion	43
	Acquisitions, take-overs and risk arbitrage	43
	Settlement	45
	The new world	45

Contents

4   Commodity trading in different currencies   46
Alex McClumpha

Definition of soft commodity markets	46
The development of trading in futures	47
The oil price shocks (1971–73 and 1975–77)	48
Marketing	49
Pricing soft commodities	50
Arbitrage opportunities	52
Arbitrage dangers	54
Hedging	55
Currency risk coverage	56

5   Financial futures   58
Brian Larkman

Development of the financial futures market	58
Features of trading	60
The nature of the contracts available	62
Basic cash/futures relationships	64
Some practical considerations	70
Simple intermarket arbitrage	73
More complex strategies	75
Synthetic instruments and proxy currencies	80
Conclusion	83

6   Currency options   88
Jeryl Hack

Background	88
Currency options defined	90
Option terminology	90
Option market profiles	91
Option pricing	95
Option pricing models	98
Arbitrage in practice	100
Option trading and hedging strategies	102
Conclusion	107

7   Interest rate and currency swaps   108
Martin Bralsford

Development of the market	109
Types of swap	113
Financial evaluation of swaps	115
Credit risk in swaps	117
Legal, accounting and tax issues	117
Swaps and the corporate treasurer	119
Outlook	120

8   Cross-market arbitrage   122
   John Heywood
   Simple cash against forwards arbitrage   122
   Arbitrage using paper   125
   Arbitrage using futures   125
   Forward Rate Agreements   129
   Currency options   131
   Interest Rate Guarantees   135

Index   137

The contributors

Rudi Weisweiller (Editor). After studying Philosophy, Politics and Economics at Oxford, in 1948 he joined the merchant banking firm of J. Henry Schroder & Co. and was their Chief Foreign Exchange Dealer from 1953 until 1960. After four years with Philip Hill, Higginson, Erlangers Ltd, where he became the Manager in charge of the foreign exchange department, he set up as a currency consultant, acting as an adviser to industry and a lecturer on foreign exchange in many parts of the world. He was Managing Director of Weisweiller Adfos Ltd, which organised courses and seminars. He is the author of two books, *Foreign Exchange* (Allen & Unwin, 1972) and *Introduction to Foreign Exchange* (Woodhead-Faulkner, 1983), and of many articles on financial topics. He edited *Managing a Foreign Exchange Department: A manual of effective practice* (Woodhead-Faulkner, 1985).

Ernest Angell joined the Westminster Bank in 1938 and, after war service, became Assistant Principal in their Arbitrage Department. From 1956 he worked firstly in Canada with the Mercantile Bank and then with the Bank of London and South America in New York and later in London. He joined the Chase Manhattan Bank in 1963 and, as Vice-President, headed their dealing room. Between 1975 and 1981 he formed and headed the Treasury Division at Saudi International Bank. After subsequent service as Assistant Chief Manager at the Siam Commercial Bank's London branch, he is now Treasurer of Credito Italiano International Ltd. He is a B.Sc. (Econ) of London University.

Martin Bralsford is Director of Treasury with Cadbury Schweppes plc. He has an MSc (London) and qualified as a Chartered Accountant with Pannell Kerr Forster & Co. He is a Foundation Fellow of the Association of Corporate Treasurers of which he is a council member and a member of the editorial board publishing the Association's magazine *The Treasurer*. He is also a member of the Bank of England's Joint Standing Committee on Sterling Markets. Prior to joining Cadbury Schweppes he was Group Treasurer with the Calor Group, Group Finance Manager of the Beecham Group and then Group Treasurer of the Rank Organisation.

Jeryl L. Hack is a Vice-President of Donaldson, Lufkin & Jenrette, responsible for the London Currency Option Department. Prior to joining them in 1984, she was a Vice-President at Paine Webber International in London where she specialised in currency options and established an Institutional Currency Option Unit. From 1977 to 1982, Jeryl was with ContiCommodity Services Inc. as a Financial and Commodity Futures Broker. She holds a BS degree in International Trade and Finance from the Georgetown University School of Foreign Service.

Mungo Henderson became a member of the London Stock Exchange in 1962. He has been a jobber, a broker and a money manager. He has been director of P.C.P. (Investment Consultants) Limited since 1976 and is also now associated with T. C. Coombs and Co.

John Heywood is an Executive Director of Hambros Bank, London, where he has been responsible for the foreign exchange, Eurocurrency, futures and options trading operations since 1973. He is a frequent lecturer on these subjects and is the author of two textbooks, *Foreign Exchange and the Corporate Treasurer* (4th edition, A. & C. Black, 1984) and *Using the Futures, Forwards and Options Markets* (A. & C. Black, 1984). He is one of the four banking members of the foreign exchange market's Joint Standing Committee and is Chairman of the British Banker's Association's Currency Options Committee. Since May 1985 he has also been responsible for the computer systems of the Hambro Group. He has been with Hambro since 1969 and prior to that spent 12 years with various industrial companies, including English Electric, Esso Petroleum and PA Management Consultants. He holds a first class degree in Engineering from London University.

Brian Larkman began his banking career in 1970, having graduated from Exeter University with an honours degree in Mathematics. He held a number of posts within the Domestic Banking Division of National Westminster Bank before being appointed to the bank's newly formed financial futures unit in April 1982. He heads a team of accounts executives serving the needs of a wide cross-section of institutional, corporate and private clients. He has lectured extensively on the subject of financial futures and options in the bank's own programme of educational and marketing seminars, for LIFFE and as a guest at international conferences in London and other European centres.

Alex McClumpha is Head of Corporate Affairs at Nestlé for whom he worked in various parts of the world, including the United States and South America, before returning to take charge of purchasing in the United Kingdom in 1968. With long experience of the international markets in cocoa and coffee, he has played an active part in industry affairs. He is a past Chairman of the Coffee Terminal Market Association of London and a regular adviser to the United Kingdom and the EEC on international commodity agreements.

Ray Martine has been actively involved in securities arbitrage since 1970. After experience with a number of firms and in several markets, he presently heads the Australian Dealing Desk at T. C. Coombs and Co.

Editor's preface

When asked to write a book on arbitrage, I said that I would do so – provided someone told me what arbitrage is. This book is the result.

It is above all a practical book, but Chapter 1, What is Arbitrage?, attempts to set the scene by examining linguistic definitions and general principles. Consequently, it may have less appeal to traders in various markets than the more practical chapters which follow. It is mainly intended for those whose responsibilities include the management or supervision of risk-taking departments in the financial markets.

In attempting to clarify our ideas, the authors talked a great deal to one another. We also sought, and got, inspiration from the comments of friends and colleagues, many of whom explained their concepts to convince us of the impossibility of our task and their wisdom in not sharing it with us. Those whom I would especially wish to thank include Ginger Brooks, John Champion, Ingrid Eigenmann-von Grebmer, Bernie Furlonger, Pat Harvey, Ernest Ingold, David McWilliam, Leslie Michaels and Keith Woodbridge.

Rudi Weisweiller

CHAPTER 1

What is arbitrage?

Rudi Weisweiller

The businessman inclines, and rightly so, to the view that words should be used in accordance with market practice. Correct use to him is use in the sense in which it will be readily understood: communication relies on like interpretation of words.

In a world in which a man's or woman's word is his or her bond, the clarity of what is said is of paramount importance. Ambiguity can be seen as the worst internal enemy in the market-place.

The correct use of a word is thus a matter of practice and usage rather than of logical meaning or linguistic derivation. However, as the word 'Arbitrage' is used in different senses in different markets and often in several different senses in the same market or even by the same person at different times, an attempt at definition or at least delineation is desirable.

What can be legitimately described as arbitrage? What activities ought never to be called by that name?

If the purity of the dealer's language is not the main aim of this chapter then it is inevitable that the discussion of the word 'arbitrage' will lead us to some extent into the field of commercial morality. We shall have to suggest, however gently and hesitatingly, that some activities described as arbitrage are better than others. In making that comment the criteria will of course be commercial and not theological. They will take the profit motive as their guide and not the conscience of the individual. It is not grave sin that the arbitrageur must shun but grave risk.

Before we can usefully talk about arbitrage let us study some of the available definitions, both public and private. We quiet people in the City are largely unaware that this much-used word is vague, ambiguous and controversial. It can lead to useful debate or to dangerous misunderstandings just as words like 'love' or 'democracy' or 'freedom' often do.

The *Oxford English Dictionary* gives three definitions of arbitrage. It is, firstly, the exercise of the function of an arbiter; secondly, the exercise of individual judgement, authoritative decision or determination; and, thirdly, the traffic in bills of exchange drawn on sundry places, and bought and sold in sight of the daily quotations of rates in the several markets, each operation being based in theory on the calculation known as Arbitration of Exchange.

This in turn is defined as the determination of the rate of exchange to be obtained between two countries or currencies, when the operation is conducted through a third or several intermediate ones, in order to ascertain the most advantageous method of drawing or remitting bills.

Arbitrage is also the similar traffic in stocks, so as to take advantage of the difference of price at which the same stock may be quoted at the same time in the exchange markets of distant places.

The definition in the *Oxford English Dictionary* is remarkable in that it draws our attention to the exercise of judgement in the second definition and to the existence of relevant facts in the third. This divergence in the use of the word 'arbitrage' will occupy us later. Does he 'who transacts arbitrage business', the arbitrageur, buy and sell at known present prices in different centres and thus make money without taking a risk or does he use his judgement to try to guess correctly which way prices will move in the future? Which is arbitrage?

This same dichotomy is hinted at by the definition of arbitrageur in the 1928 edition of *Der grosse Brockhaus* which in translation describes him as a bank employee who deals with arbitrage business and who needs technical know-how, ability to take decisions and mathematical accuracy.

The word has at its root the French *arbitrer* and this in turn comes from the Latin *arbitrium*. In Freund & Lewis (1984 edition) this is translated as the judgement or decision of an arbitrator, who is described as a master, ruler, lord, umpire or judge. Arbitration was seen even in Roman days as referring to judgement, opinion and decision rather than a simply legal ruling, so that terms like mastery, dominion, authority, power, free will were deemed appropriate to this concept. Again, we are put on notice that the simple mechanical utilisation of temporary price divergences in different places is not all that arbitrage is about.

All indications point to the suggestion that arbitrage activities combine knowledge and foresight in a subtle harmony, perhaps recalling the definition of genius as being 1% inspiration and 99% perspiration. There is however no evidence in favour of the ingenious claim that the word 'arbitrage' is derived from *Arbeit*, the German word for work, underlining the necessary blend between factual information and intellectual effort required by the successful arbitrageur.

The German reference work *Duden* (Vol. 1 of the ten-volume 18th Edition, 1980) simply describes arbitrage as the exploiting (*Ausnützen*) of differences in prices on different exchanges. This presumably covers currency markets as well as stock exchanges. It leaves open the purpose of this exploitation.

This is stated a little more clearly in the 1928 edition of *Larousse du XXe Siècle* where arbitrage is defined as follows: 'Achat d'une marchandise, d'une valeur de Bourse, d'une lettre de change, sur un marché, en négociation de ladite sur un autre marché où le cours est plus élevé'. (Purchase of goods, shares or currency drafts in one market for sale of same in another market where the price is higher.) This list is matched by one in *Meyers Konversationslexikon* (6th Edition, 1902) where *Geldarbitrage* (money), *Wechselarbitrage* (drafts) and *Diskontarbitrage* (discount or interest rates) are mentioned. Motivation here clearly is the making of a profit out of the combined deals. The above-quoted edition of Larousse however goes on to say: 'L'arbitrage a pour conséquence le nivellement et l'équilibre des prix'. (Arbitrage has as its consequences the levelling of prices and their equilibrium.)

It is an inevitable consequence of successful, that is to say profitable, arbitrage in any area that prices will reach the same level and then be in equilibrium. Two comments are appropriate at this stage and need always to be borne in mind by all those engaged in arbitrage activities. Firstly, when arbitrage has been done, price differences will have vanished and further profitable arbitrage in the same values is no longer possible. One of the essential qualities of the good arbitrageur is therefore the ability to know or guess or sense the size operation which is neither bigger nor smaller than the offers and bids which at any particular moment are found to be in disequilibrium and therefore ready for his attention.

The second comment concerns motivation. Arbitrageurs operate for profit. This is their motive. Arbitrage also has a second and perhaps more important consequence, which is the levelling out of prices and the re-establishment of overall market equilibrium. Without the skill and courage of the arbitrageur this will not be achieved. His activity has a social value in a free market and there is no substitute for it. The authorities are thus wise to allow and even encourage such activities, but the would-be arbitrageur must not allow the social and economic value of his successful operations to blind him to the financial risks involved. For not all arbitrage is free of risk.

Before discussing in more detail the many and varied activities which are at times covered by the term 'arbitrage' it is enlightening to observe the evolution of the term over the years.

The 1910 edition of the *Encyclopaedia Britannica* quotes extensively foreign exchange opportunities in the year 1906. They show profit to the arbitrageur without necessarily leading to an equalising of prices. It is clear that fixed exchange rates curtail arbitrage opportunities and that floating rates create them. In any market, the possibility of violent and frequent movements in prices tends to open up opportunities for the arbitrageur. The more the markets have a free rate structure without government interference, the more inter-market opportunities for arbitrage will be found. Rapidity and reliability of information around the world is of course the biggest factor limiting arbitrage opportunities, although this is frequently overstated. Even the most efficient system of communications cannot tell everybody everything at once: the intelligent operator will continue to find significant price disequilibria if he knows where and how to look for them.

The 1962 edition of the *Encyclopaedia Britannica* leads us a good bit further into the evolving use of the word: 'Arbitrage is the term applied to the *system* of equalizing prices in different commercial centres by buying in the cheaper market and selling in the dearer. These transactions . . . are carried on between the various financial centres of the world.' It goes on to express an important commercial truth which removes arbitrage from some earlier definitions of riskless market operations (like those of 1906 described in the 1910 edition): 'The scale of profit on arbitrage transactions varies with the risks entailed'. The older definition however suffices to justify a further comment in the same edition: 'To be a successful arbitrageur it is of vital importance to be well informed, to be quick so as to get in before one's competitors and to have a reliable and energetic counterparty'. There are those who would question the need for energy in one's counterparty beyond a normal willingness to trade.

The 1983 version of the 15th edition of the *Encyclopaedia Britannica* describes arbitrage as a business operation involving purchase of foreign exchange, gold, securities or commodities in one market and their almost simultaneous sale in another market. This is of course the most traditional definition and does not seem to cover many of the activities involving judgement and risk which are in fact described as arbitrage at the present time. The *Encyclopaedia* goes on to say that arbitrage generally tends to eliminate price differences between markets. We are then reminded that such activities take place between different villages in less developed countries whereas in highly developed countries arbitrage generally refers to international operations involving foreign exchange rates, short-term interest rates, the price of gold and the price of securities. One wonders to what extent even in developed countries the exploitation of price variations between different shops and supermarkets or the utilisation of differences in customs duties and in levels of value added tax in neighbouring states ought not to be covered by the term 'arbitrage'.

Indeed this idea that shopping around between markets is also a form of arbitrage (as distinct from buying in one market and selling at a profit in another) was included in the definition of arbitrage in the 15th edition of *Der grosse Brockhaus* in 1928: 'the choice of the most favourable out of the several available possibilities when buying or selling or making payments'.

Motivation is clearly an important albeit confused aspect in many definitions of arbitrage. So far we have tended to look at situations in which profit can be made from arbitrage transactions, with or without the risks inherent in taking a view or in speculation, or those in which costs can be reduced by arbitrage. It is however clear that the term arbitrage is also applied to hedging. Here the aim is insurance against loss. Commodity hedging, for instance, can be described as the concluding of deals which will exclude or limit the risks on the physical transaction by entering into a corresponding transaction in a futures market. The consequence of this must be largely to offset any loss on the one by a profit on the other or vice versa.

Before leaving the published definitions in books of reference and turning to quotations from actual operators in the market, it is worthwhile looking at an English rendering of the very full definition of arbitrage which appeared in the 1928 edition of *Larousse*.

1. One calls arbitrage an operation on an Exchange where stocks or goods are sold and bought. This operation is based on *unjustified* differences in the rates either on the same Exchange between similar titles or on

different Exchanges between the rates for the same stock or the same goods. Arbitraging these stocks or goods is accordingly to sell at the higher price where it is more expensive so as to buy it more cheaply where it is less expensive. Thus the demand grows for that which is *unjustly* depreciated on the Exchange where it is depreciated; the offer for that which is overvalued grows on the Exchange where it is overvalued; and by the game of offer and bid which is the consequence of arbitrage transactions, the unjustified differences in rates tend to lessen and then to disappear. At the same time, anyone who sells the stock or the goods more dearly where they are overvalued to buy them more cheaply where they are undervalued makes a profit. On the Exchanges certain banking firms specialise in the practice of arbitrage, establishing a connection between different Exchanges all over the world and securing a definite identity of rates between them; these are the arbitrage banks.

2. Arbitrage thus understood grows in importance during troubled times when rates between different countries are unstable. On the one hand, it acquires a new target, occupying itself with foreign currencies and notes in a way which assures similar prices on the Exchanges in different countries. On the other hand, it combines on these different Exchanges the rates for different goods and stocks with the rates of exchange for the currencies in which they are traded in such a way as to make apparent among the actual prices of transactions the differences which warrant arbitrage.

3. One calls 'international stocks' those which are quoted on the Exchanges of different countries and therefore lend themselves better than others to the practice of arbitrage.

4. Arbitrage transactions can be used in manifold combinations. They can be made for spot or forward delivery. Spot arbitrage consists of exchanging stocks one holds in one's portfolio against other stocks which seem safer or promise higher returns; hence the name portfolio arbitrage. Fixed date forward arbitrage consists of selling such stocks forward and buying others for the same value date in the *expectation* of a drop in the price of the former *and* an increase in the price of the latter.

5. Arbitrage is often done between one place and another; it would then not concern different stocks but the same stocks quoted on different Exchanges. The word parity is used to describe the situation created by the equivalence of rates in two different places. This kind of operation has become very difficult because of changes in exchange rates.

6. Contango arbitrage consists of carrying settlement for one's stocks forward at a good price and buying other stocks with the money thus made available.

7. One also uses the word arbitrage to describe operations by which commercial brokers confirm or deny conformity of goods delivered with specifications or samples and stipulate, if they have reason to, a reduction in the purchase price called rebate. Arbitrage on goods is much used not only in domestic trade, where it serves to enable traders to

cover themselves against price instabilities, but also in international trade where commodities like cereals, coffee and cotton lend themselves to a variety of speculative operations.

The last paragraph of the *Larousse* definition is confusing. It refers to the work of brokers who perform the function of arbitrator. This takes us right back to the Roman definition of a quasi-judicial function in which the law is interpreted with the help of superior knowledge and mature judgement. The paragraph however moves on to hedging and then to the use of arbitrage as an exercise in risk taking.

A more interesting aspect of the *Larousse* definition is the use of curiously emotive words like *injustifiées* and *injustement* in the first paragraph and *prévision* in the fourth. Is there a connection between the professional 'expectation' in the fourth paragraph (based presumably on the correct exercise of individual judgement envisaged by the *Oxford English Dictionary*) and the pompous description of a particular price as 'unjustified' in the first paragraph? This raises the same problems as the frequent use of the words 'overvalued' and 'undervalued' by foreign exchange dealers when really saying no more than that they believe the price of a currency will go down or up.

The scope of this book is arbitrage in those areas which involve the use of different currencies as part of the arbitrage operation. Each author will make or imply his or her own definition of the term. The very divergence of these definitions sustains the widespread interest in the subject at the present time.

By way of further comment some contemporary uses of the word in the markets of today are worth looking at.

One very elegant definition is 'the process by which a perceived gap in a specific area is closed by the intelligent use of resources in various areas'. Another definition offered by an experienced practitioner is 'the simultaneous buying and selling of instruments (identical or not) in order to take advantage of known price discrepancies'. 'Arbitrage is normally', according to another professional, 'a series of riskless transactions undertaken to take advantage of price or yield differentials in different markets'. Even in operations perceived as riskless, the credit risk in respect of different counterparties has got to be taken into account.

A slightly more academic attempt to cover much of what people in fact describe as arbitrage lists three types: firstly, purchase in one centre and sale in another; secondly, purchase from one institution and sale to another in the same centre, which presupposes that the two institutions can't or won't deal with one another direct; and thirdly, transactions involving two markets, as is the case with all interest arbitrage and with the opportunities described in the last chapter of this book.

Although an extreme view of language accepts any use of words, however unusual or strange, which is indulged in by anyone, this does not make for clarity in communication. For this reason one can perhaps deem as outside the scope of this book the definition in the administrative set-up of one major bank on the Continent of arbitrage as meaning inter-bank spot currency trading (as opposed to interbank forward trading or Eurocurrency deposits or foreign exchange deals with corporate customers).

Likewise, it may not be helpful to attempt to define arbitrage in accord with a recent newspaper comment: 'The profits of the Group came from investment dealing, reflecting everyday risk arbitrage in certain shares'. Chapter 3, on stock arbitrage, gives a clearer definition.

It should by now be clear that the word 'arbitrage' is sometimes used to cover some activities which clearly do not deserve this term and should be given a less spectacular name. Dealing in the market is sometimes the more accurate term, making no claim to greater knowledge or deeper insight than is the normal attribute of any respectable trader.

At the other extreme are the activities of pure arbitrage, which have a flavour of fairy-tale ingenuity and often evoke memories of inadequate communications long since reformed by contemporary technology. The silver arbitrage between London and Shanghai before November 1935 seems to fit into this nostalgic memory of the clever discovery and riskless exploitation of unjustified price discrepancies. So does the happy recollection of a young foreign exchange dealer in the 1950s who bought forward French francs against sterling in Paris and sold them against guilders in Amsterdam, only to find that on several occasions the guilders thus acquired fetched in London more sterling than the amount he had committed a few minutes earlier.

Between these two extremes, which one could call bogus arbitrage and pure arbitrage, we must place a great variety of transactions which are properly called arbitrage although not entirely free of risk.

The delineation which answers the question posed in the heading for this introductory chapter will find its full answer only in the pages of the other chapters. Here, a more general answer serves our purpose better; it takes the form of comment on arbitrage rather than definition of it.

Arbitrage is essentially a private matter. Its successful performance depends on knowledge which is either unknowable to others or undiscovered by others. While this is a valid assertion and the very starting point for the eager arbitrageur, he ought never to underestimate the talents and persistence of professional colleagues in other institutions. They too may acquire knowledge and find ways which, strictly speaking, are the birthright of a genius like himself. Bitter experience has taught many of us that the perceived gap can vanish before we have completed the necessary deals if others have equally good eyesight and nimbler limbs.

Some opportunities, and we must never stop looking for them, come to us from an advantage which other practitioners in the same market do not have. There may be balance-sheet constraints which prevent them from doing certain transactions. The non-availability to others of space within limits, whether for specific counterparties or countries or certain popular maturities, inevitably provides opportunities for arbitrage to the few who at that particular moment are not so constrained. Some opportunities too will only be usable by those dealers who already have fixed lines and limits in wise expectation of future opportunities. Where major speculative pressures on any set of market rates are foreseen and prepared for, arbitrage opportunities may in fact be available only to the well-prepared minority of dealers.

Exchange control, however undesirable as a concept and however constraining to trade and investment also, provides frequent arbitrage opportunities. The impact of the relevant rules on different types of operators needs careful study. Differential exchange rates have often brought interesting opportunities to those with knowledge of financial francs or rands or the blocked accounts of many countries with balance of payments problems.

A good example of such arbitrage activities is clearly summarised in the following memorandum written early in 1963:

'A UK resident holding South African securities in South Africa may if he wishes have them exported to the United Kingdom and sell them on any recognised stock exchange.

SA securities whilst held in South Africa must be held by a bank or a stock exchange, the certificates being endorsed 'Non-Resident held'. They may be sold on a local stock exchange to a local resident who is able to cancel this endorsement. The proceeds of such a sale are credited to a blocked SA rand account in the name of the non-resident.

Blocked rand held for non-residents of South Africa cannot be transferred from one account to another. They can however be used for the purchase of other South African shares for the same client, but when these new shares are resold the proceeds are once again credited to a blocked rand account.

Although blocked rand are not transferrable, non-resident owned securities held in South Africa may be transferred to another non-resident.

Accordingly non-residents can dispose of their blocked rand at a discount of approximately $12\frac{1}{2}\%$ (2.28 SA rand = £1) in the following manner:

The non-resident contacts a London arbitrageur, who arranges on his behalf the purchase of securities in South Africa against his blocked rand. The non-resident then instructs the South African stockbroker to transfer his stock to the account of the London arbitrageur. The London arbitrageur then sells the stock for blocked rand, which he uses for his genuine investment orders. He pays the equivalent to his non-resident client in free funds after taking into account expenses which he has incurred in the various transactions.'

Many a definition of arbitrage in the different financial markets uses phrases like 'deals simultaneously struck'. This is the purest version of the great multitude of transactions covered by arbitrageurs. The extent to which we deviate from this concept in either time or certainty is the measure on the one hand of the risk to which we allow ourselves to be exposed and on the other hand of the magnitude of profit (or loss) which we might incur.

In this way, arbitrage (except the rare but highly desirable breed of absolute purity) follows the normal and proper rules of the market-place: the greater the risk, the bigger the profit or loss which will result.

Where then lies the attraction of arbitrage? Surely in this: that the conscientious dealer will seek to be not luckier nor even cleverer than his peers, but consistently harder-working and more vigilant. He will also use his experience and his brains to control his fancies and to train his professional judgement. Thus eagerness is coupled with restraint and enterprise with realism.

The key rules for the good arbitrageur, the arbitrageur who consistently earns for his employer or institution more than he loses, and risks less than he has made, are the following:

1. Look for opportunities, in your own market and all related markets, at busy times and at quiet times, where they were found before and also where nobody expects to find them, for all maturities and in every country.
2. Learn to differentiate between paper possibilities and real ones, because the former are plentiful and unrealisable and the latter are rare and much sought after.
3. Be the best-informed man or woman in your market and exploit your knowledge with wisdom, energy and courage.

And does this not give us at least a tentative answer to the question 'What is Arbitrage?' It is the professional search for and pursuit of rate differences already known and usable, or reasonably expected to occur in the near future, with limited risk and on a relatively moderate scale, so as to achieve a steady profit. The incidental but important consequence of this is to improve markets worldwide by equalising prices available to all. Exceptional returns are only within the reach of those with special knowledge or opportunities.

CHAPTER 2

Interest arbitrage

Ernest Angell

The underlying concept

For 'interest arbitrage', as it is now generally understood in the money markets, the underlying concept is the movement of funds *from one currency to another* for the sake of an improvement in the yield. If one is a borrower the yield is a cost which one pays and so a reduction is an improvement; if one is a lender the yield is income and so the converse applies.

Our concern is with the money markets in which moneys are borrowed and lent in varying ways. Here yield can be expressed as interest accruing on a starting principal at a percentage rate per annum. Alternatively it can be expressed as a discount at a percentage rate per annum deducted at the outset from the face value of an instrument and amortised thereafter. Before alternative yields may legitimately be compared it is essential to express both in the same way; and it is customary to express all comparative yields as interest. 'Discount to yield' is the conventional expression for this.

Internationally, percentage interest rates per annum are generally quoted on a 360-day base. At the rate of 1%, each day earns 1/360th of 1%. In the United Kingdom the conventional base for sterling is still 365 days; and so each day earns only 1/365th of 1% which is a little bit less than that earned on a 360-day base. Thus it is also important to express interest yields on the same base before making comparisons.

Naturally it is perfectly valid to think of interest arbitrage within a single currency especially if there is a money market for that currency in more than one centre. Certainly there is such a market for a number of currencies, with the US dollar predominant amongst them, and market-making dealers do take advantage of such opportunities when they arise. This simply means that moneys are borrowed for a particular term from one centre or source at a certain rate and contemporaneously re-lent elsewhere at a slightly higher rate. But this type of money market arbitrage is subsumed under the general heading of 'trading' or 'dealing'. In this case the interest differential is synonymous with the 'jobber's turn' which is the difference between the bid and the offer sides of the market-maker's each way quotation.

The term 'interest arbitrage', or alternatively 'time arbitrage', is sometimes used to describe a rather different type of operation. Here money is borrowed, or lent, for a particular period of time with the resultant cash flow being offset by a lending or a borrowing for a different period. Given a normal upward-sloping interest rate curve a simultaneous borrowing at one month's term and a lending at six months' will show a profit, at least over the first month. A reverse operation on an untypical downward-sloping rate curve would yield a similar result. But this type of operation involves taking a risk position on both the level and the shape of the interest rate curve for the period from the end of the first month to the end of the sixth. Whilst such mismatched risk positions in terms of interest rate sensitivity are part of every money trader's business they are not an interest arbitrage activity within our concept of that activity. Extraneous risks, such as interest rate fluctuations, are to be avoided.

It goes without saying that, for the betterment of a yield to be a valid arbitrage concept, the quality of the liability and asset on each side has to be as nearly as possible identical. On this basis one may validly arbitrage between US and UK Treasury Bills, or between bank deposits where the institutions are of comparable quality, or between their CDs (certificates of deposits), or between the bills of exchange which they have accepted. But where there is any difference in credit quality or instrument between the two sides of the arbitrage an allowance for this 'product differentiation' is required when evaluating the arbitrage.

As a result, interest arbitrages are usually assessed in the first instance by using, as a common form of reference, the London Inter-Bank Offered Rates (LIBOR) quoted in the market. These are the interest rates at which banks in London *offer* deposits in internationally traded currencies to their counterparts in London and elsewhere. The LIBOR rates quoted at 11 a.m. have come to be accepted as the governing form of reference in Europe. There are also LIBID rates which are the *bid* sides of the same rates, and LIMEAN rates which are the mid points between the two. There is a similar concept in other time zones, in both New York and Singapore.

Thus we have the concept that, once it is properly set up, interest arbitrage provides the betterment in yield across two currencies whilst leaving no extraneous risks outstanding. In fact the only outstanding risk is in the credit quality of the instruments or contracts used in the arbitrage; these will be discussed later in this chapter.

But is this really the case? Moving funds between two currencies involves exchange risks, and the expression 'interest arbitrage' is loosely used to describe many currency transfers with an interest betterment motive where the exchange risk has not itself been eliminated; such transfers are uncovered interest arbitrages.

Uncovered interest arbitrage

The dominant factor on the world scene over the past year or two has been the enormous flow of funds into the US dollar with amounts aggregating many billions of dollars. The attraction has been, and continues to be, the relatively high interest rate structure and the relatively low rate of inflation in the United States. The counterpart has been the growing American balance of payments deficit with the rest of the world which the inflow has financed. Moneys have been attracted to the United States from all quarters of the globe, and in particular from Japan which some had regarded as an 'immature' creditor country, that is, a country which is still only building up its foreign asset base. It will not be immature much longer.

Interest rate comparisons

Some indicative quotations (current at the end of October 1985) for bank deposits of wholesale size at six months' term in several different internationally traded currencies illustrate the wide range of yields available:

	% per annum		*% per annum*
Swiss francs	$4\frac{5}{8}$	US dollars	$8\frac{1}{8}$
Deutschmarks	5	ECUs	$8\frac{3}{4}$
Guilders	$6\frac{1}{4}$	French francs	$10\frac{3}{4}$
Yen	$7\frac{3}{8}$	£ sterling	$11\frac{1}{2}$

Notwithstanding the higher yields offered by both Paris and London for their local currencies, the significant flows have been into the US dollar. Thus a favourable interest differential is not in itself sufficient to attract depositors especially if this differential is accompanied by a perception of a weakness in the currency which may lead to its depreciation on the exchanges. As a composite, but not yet a currency, the ECU (European Currency Unit) does offer a better prospect of a relatively low volatility in its exchange value against the European Monetary System currencies of which it is composed. The ECU is still in the early stages of its development and it does not yet attract any great inflow in spite of its interest rate advantage and comparative stability in European terms.

The contrast with the dollar is total as America has the largest, deepest and broadest financial markets so far experienced anywhere. The opportunities for investment there are varied and widespread; and one need not imagine that the vast volumes of funds moving into the United States have done so simply on the strength of the interest rate differential on bank deposits.

Uncovered exchange risks

Manifestly the exchange risk has not been covered on the bulk of the funds which have been shifted into the dollar, and the uncovered funds are subject to loss, not merely of income but also of capital, if the exchange rate of the dollar depreciates in terms of the investor's home currency.

None the less the six months' bank deposit market can provide a simple example from which to quantify the exchange risk for an investor who gives up the opportunity to earn, say, $7\frac{3}{8}\%$ per annum in yen in order to enjoy the higher yield of $8\frac{1}{8}\%$ per annum in US dollars.

Example:
A deposit of US$1 million at this rate will grow to US$1,040,625 over six months and at a spot rate of around ¥210 per dollar the initial exchange into

dollars would cost the depositor ¥210 million which, over half a year, would have grown to ¥217,743,750 at the rate indicated of $7\frac{3}{8}\%$ per annum. Were the exchange rate of ¥210 to remain unchanged at the end of the half-year when the US$1,040,625 was available for re-conversion into yen, the product would be ¥218,531,250 to show a gain of ¥787,500. This gain is equivalent to an interest yield of $\frac{3}{4}\%$ per annum on the ¥210 million invested; and this additional return represents the interest differential between the yen interest rate of $7\frac{3}{8}\%$ per annum and that for dollars of $8\frac{1}{8}\%$ per annum.

However, if the ¥210 has changed at the end of the six months the yen product will be different from that given above; and the difference will be either a windfall gain or a windfall loss for the originating yen investor. If the exchange value of the dollar has risen in yen terms over the period it will be worth more than ¥210 at the end. The investor will then recover more yen than anticipated and so have a windfall gain. By contrast, if the dollar has depreciated against the yen, it will buy fewer yen and so give a smaller product. The investor is then facing a windfall loss.

This loss will not necessarily be limited to the loss of all or part of the motivating $\frac{3}{4}\%$ per annum interest differential. It may produce a loss which erodes part or all of the $7\frac{3}{8}\%$ per annum that could have been earned had the deposit been left in yen. The loss can indeed go still further and produce at the out-turn a smaller amount of yen than the ¥210 million invested at the start. This is the loss of part of the capital invested as well as of all the income.

In terms of exchange rates a fall in the dollar's value from ¥210.00 to ¥209.24 will completely erode the interest differential and leave the investor no better off than he would have been without the arbitrage. A drop to ¥201.80 will wipe out all the income and simply return the ¥210 million to the investor without any income for the six months. Any further fall below this level would start to eat into the principal invested. A rate of ¥192.19 would return only ¥200 million to the investor who would thereby have lost ¥10 million, which is a *negative* interest rate of 10% per annum on his ¥210 million investment

By the same token, a borrower needing dollars who, attracted by the lower interest rate, had elected to borrow yen instead and then exchanged them for dollars, would face the same risk profile. If, when the time for repayment arrived, the dollar had appreciated against the yen, a windfall profit would be made as fewer dollars would need to be re-exchanged in order to repay the yen principal and the interest due on it. *Per contra*, a decline in exchange value of the dollar against the yen would produce a windfall loss in terms of an enhanced borrowing cost.

As in the investment example above, if the exchange rate remains at ¥210 per dollar, the six months' borrowing of US$1 million will have cost only $7\frac{3}{8}\%$ per annum for it will require only US$1,036,875 to purchase the ¥217,743,750 needed to repay the yen principal plus interest. If the dollar falls to ¥209.24 it will take US$1,040,641 to repay the borrowing. The interest rate cost is $8\frac{1}{8}\%$ per annum and there is no advantage in having borrowed yen rather than dollars. Should the dollar fall further to the lower level of ¥201.80 repayment would require US$1,079,008 for a dollar interest rate cost of 15.80% per annum; and a drop to the lowest level mentioned of ¥192.19 would produce a payment requirement of US$1,132,961 for an interest rate at the usurious level of 26.59% per annum.

In comparison with the fluctuations seen in recent years in a number of other exchanges, the volatility of the dollar's value in terms of yen has been relatively modest. In the first ten months of 1985 this value declined from around ¥250 to about ¥210. A drop of ¥40 at this level is one of 16% and, as the foregoing example shows, proportionately smaller falls are more than enough to vitiate an interest rate arbitrage which includes an uncovered exchange risk. From ¥210 the fall to ¥209.24 is one of 0.36%; to ¥201.80 it is 3.90%; and even to ¥192.19 it is no more than 8.48%.

Possible acceptance of exchange risk

It is fair to remind oneself that, if the underlying exchange speculation is successful, the risk taken in combining an interest rate arbitrage with an open exchange position will produce an additional profit which enhances the interest rate betterment implicit in the interest arbitrage itself. On the other hand the simple foregoing example suffices to demonstrate the very real risks of loss should the exchange speculation go awry.

In recent years the volatility of exchange rates in general has been such as to discourage the acceptance of open-ended exchange risks in situations in which they can be avoided. If it is desired to run exchange risks with a view to earning profits it is far preferable to manage the relevant open exchange positions as business operations in their own right; and not to mix them up with differently conceived activities such as interest arbitrage.

Longer term exchange risk

In practice it is the non-banking sectors, rather than the banking sector itself, which tend towards uncovered interest arbitrage: those who save, or collect savings, in one currency and invest them in another; or those who borrow in one currency and disburse the loans in another. As the maturities for such operations tend to be medium or longer term they can most readily be thought of as capital market transactions whether or not they are formulated in instruments for which traded markets exist.

For such transactions the open exchange position is normally accepted as a risk which has to be borne when implementing interest arbitrages at medium to longer term. The risk may turn out well and so increase the interest rate betterment in the uncovered arbitrage. Exchange risk cover for these longer periods is considered difficult, complex and expensive. In any event it is bound to eliminate most if not all of the interest rate differential which looks so attractive when the exchange risk is left uncovered.

For more percipient operators it is, however, sometimes possible to combine short-term exchange cover with an underlying longer-term position; and this can be helpful when the markets first scent a shift in an existing relationship pattern between currencies. Over the past few years the world has become accustomed to the concept of a relatively overvalued US dollar with the accompanying undervaluation of the currencies with which the dollar is exchanged, particularly of the yen. However, this concept is changing at the time of writing. The new feeling is that the dollar's perceived overvaluation may be removed by its depreciation on the exchanges. The governments of the United States, Japan, Germany, France and the United Kingdom have announced the desirability of such a development; and they are attempting to lean their weight in that direction in both the money and the exchange markets. The exchange value of the dollar has already obliged by showing some recent decline against most other important currencies. (See note on page 31.)

Problems of exchange risk acceptance

Amongst those for whom this poses a problem are Japanese investors in US dollar bonds; and there are plenty of them. A currently representative yield for US Treasury ten-year notes is $10\frac{1}{8}\%$ per annum. Forward yen are at a premium over forward dollars on the exchanges and, to quote from the indicative interest rate levels mentioned earlier, a yen purchase against dollars for delivery in six months' time would carry a cost equivalent to the difference in these levels, i.e. $\frac{3}{4}\%$ per annum. Thus the cost of protecting the bond portfolio against dollar depreciation against the yen over the next six months is the equivalent of a reduction in the bond yield from $10\frac{1}{8}\%$ to $9\frac{3}{8}\%$ per annum.

This does not seem to be an exorbitant price but it does involve a commitment to sell dollars and buy yen for delivery in six months' time at a rate of ¥209.24 which is somewhat under the current spot price of ¥210.00. Moreover the exchange risk re-emerges in six months' time when dollars have to be delivered in settlement of the forward sale. There is no guarantee that the price of the dollar bonds will itself be maintained so the dollars required to meet the forward sale may not then be available from the sale of the bonds. Nor is there any suggestion that the investor will necessarily wish to sell the bonds in six months' time, or indeed now.

None the less dollars must be found for delivery under the forward sale contract when it matures. If these are not to come from the bond sale they must be bought in the market at the rate then ruling – which is currently unknown. The dollars thus bought can then be offset against the dollars due for delivery under the maturing forward contract with a net cash settlement equivalent to the difference between the then spot rate and the rate of ¥209.24 fixed now under the forward contract. If the dollar's yen value rises above ¥209.24 there will be a loss; if it falls below, a profit.

If the dollar's exchange value does rise in terms of yen this may be because interest yields on dollar bonds have risen relative to the comparable yields on Japanese bonds. A rise in dollar yields would normally depress the market value of the bonds themselves. A valuation loss on the bonds would then have to be taken into account on top of the realised loss on 'closing out' the forward dollar sale contract.

Arbitrage

On the other hand, if the dollar's yen value falls this may indicate a declining dollar interest rate level in relation to that of Japan. The gain on 'closing out' the forward dollar sale is then likely to be reinforced by a capital gain in bond portfolio as prices rise in response to the decline in yield.

Fully covered interest arbitrage

Extremely wide and persistent fluctuations in exchange rates between major currencies have been experienced in the markets over the years since 1971 when the US dollar was first freed from its earlier 'fixed parity' concept and allowed to 'float' with its exchange value determined by market forces. Partiality for floating and thus for potentially volatile exchange rates may now be waning; but, as long as it exists, it will force attention on the elimination of the exchange risk when moneys are transferred from one currency to another.

Interest arbitrage to seek a betterment in the yield factor is a prime motive for switching currencies. Covering the open exchange risk on such a switch involves a re-exchange at a fixed rate on a future date back into the currency which has been sold in the first instance. The forward exchange markets and the currency futures markets offer the 'products' by the use of which the exchange risk may be covered.

Understandably the hedging technique involves a cost; and, with the cost basically determined by the interest rate differential between the two currencies, most, if not all, of that differential will be absorbed in the cost. The risk of exchange loss will have been covered. The chance of an exchange gain will, however, have been eliminated along with the interest differential.

The 'round robin'

To demonstrate what happens a simplified example is set up in Table 2.1 in the form of a 'round robin'. The underlying formulae are now incorporated in most modern computer systems which handle exchange dealing; and many programmable calculators are capable of handling them too. The description 'round robin' indicates that the formulation is internally consistent.

For simple interest arbitrage there are only three variables: the two interest rates, one for each currency, and the differential between the two exchange rates, one for each date. Given any two variables, the third is determined and the internal consistency is shown by the fact that one can work the formulation in any desired direction. One can work from the spot to the forward, or vice versa; from the bought side to the sold, or vice versa; or from the borrowed side to that lent, or vice versa. As a matter of convention it is usual to start in the top row with the currency purchased at the nearer, or spot, date on the left-hand side. The bottom row then necessarily has the same currency on the left-hand side but this time the amount is that sold for the further, or forward, date. As with all conventions this is simply a matter of choice, but consistency in this matter does simplify administrative control.

Table 2.1. 'Round robin' for a six months' covered interest arbitrage.

Transaction	US dollars	Exchange ¥ per $	Transaction	Yen
Spot purchase	1,000,000	210.00	Spot sale	210,000,000
Interest at $8\frac{1}{8}$% p.a.	40,625	(0.76)	Interest at $7\frac{3}{8}$% p.a.	7,743,750
6 months' sale	1,040,625	209,24	6 months' purchase	217,743,750

Table 2.1 uses the rates quoted earlier and shows US$1 million growing at $8\frac{1}{8}$% per annum to become US$1,040,625 whilst the ¥210 million increases at $7\frac{3}{8}$% per annum to ¥217,743,750. The dollar principal has grown somewhat faster than the yen and, at the end of the six months, there are relatively more dollars than there are yen. Clearly there is an equivalence here. ¥210 million are worth US$1 million on the spot, and ¥217,743,750 are worth US$1,040,625 in six months' time. The six months' forward exchange rate, in yen per dollar, is simply this ¥217,743,750 divided by US$1,040,625; that is, ¥209.24. It is readily observable that, at six months' term, the dollar is somewhat less valuable in terms of yen than it is on the spot. This is logical as their differing interest rates have generated relatively more dollars than yen over the period. In the yen/dollar exchange the forward dollar thus stands at a discount against the spot. Alternatively one may say that the forward yen is at a premium against the spot. It costs relatively more dollars to buy yen six months' forward then it does to buy them on the spot.

Each of the three variables in the 'round robin' has its own market-place. There is a market for dollar deposits, and another for yen, in both of which interest rates are quoted on a percentage per annum basis. There is a third market for foreign exchange 'swaps' between dollars and yen in which the quotations are made in terms of the differential between the two exchange rates. In all three markets the quotations will be made on a jobbing basis; that is with rates for the bid side which differ somewhat from those on the offered side. This spread is the classical 'jobbers turn'. In Table 2.1 middle rates have been used from the two deposit markets with the result that the foreign exchange swap margin which is derived from them is also a middle rate. In the real world the quotations given by the makers of these three markets are much more likely to look something like this:

	Offered	Bid
US dollar deposits: % per annum	$8\frac{3}{16}$	$8\frac{1}{16}$
Japanese yen deposits: % per annum	$7\frac{7}{16}$	$7\frac{5}{16}$
Dollar swaps: discount per $	¥0.63	¥0.88

The forward dollar is at a discount against the yen and so the market-maker offering to sell it in exchange for the spot dollar will do so with less discount than that which he quotes for the reverse operation.

As already shown, a potential covered interest arbitrageur knows before he contemplates these bid and offer quotations that the cost of the exchange cover will absorb most of the $\frac{7}{8}$ to $\frac{5}{8}$% per annum differential between the

Arbitrage

two deposit rates. But none of the rates for the three variables is fixed. The prices quoted for them will vary somewhat from time to time during the day, and indeed from market-place to market-place. The arbitrageur's objective will therefore be to secure one or more of the variables at quotations which show an acceptable margin for the arbitrage. Expressed in interest terms an acceptable margin may be anything from $\frac{1}{16}$ to $\frac{1}{4}$% per annum but in markets as active as those for dollars and for yen it is hardly likely to be more. A few 'round robins' from different points of view may clarify the possibilities.

A first example might be of someone needing dollars for which, on the rates quoted above, he would face a cost of $8\frac{3}{16}$% per annum for the six months. The same person may have yen available for employment for six months, and for these he could expect to earn $7\frac{5}{16}$% per annum. Were he instead to swap these yen into dollars for six months, a discount of ¥0.88 per dollar would be suffered on the forward dollar sale. Table 2.2 sets up the 'round robin'. Nothing has been gained and the operation is pointless.

Table 2.2. 'Round robin' for a six months' covered interest arbitrage.

Transaction	US dollars	Exchange ¥ per $	Transaction	Yen
Spot purchase	1,000,000	210.00	Spot sale	210,000,000
Interest at $8\frac{3}{16}$% p.a.	40,924	(0.88)	Interest at $7\frac{5}{16}$% p.a.	7,678,125
Forward sale	1,040,924	209,12	Forward sale	217,678,125

However, if the arbitrageur can find a swap quotation which is somewhat less than the ¥0.88 discount, then a possible betterment is discernible. Table 2.3 sets up the 'round robin' for the swap margin of ¥0.76 which was used in Table 2.1.

Table 2.3. 'Round robin' for a six months' covered interest arbitrage.

Transaction	US dollars	Exchange ¥ per $	Transaction	Yen
Spot purchase	1,000,000	210.00	Spot sale	210,000,000
Interest at $8\frac{1}{16}$% p.a.	40,312.50	(0.76)	Interest at $7\frac{5}{16}$% p.a.	7,678,125
Forward sale	1,040,312.50	209.24	Forward sale	217,678,125

Here yen, on which $7\frac{5}{16}$% per annum could have been earned, have been used to fund dollars at $8\frac{1}{16}$% per annum which would otherwise have cost $8\frac{3}{16}$% per annum. This is a worthwhile improvement of $\frac{1}{8}$% per annum. The arbitrage is justified.

With this particular combination of interest and exchange rates, and just as a matter of coincidence, it may readily be seen that a margin of ¥0.06 per dollar in the forward margin is pretty well the equivalent of $\frac{1}{16}$% per annum (0.0625) in the differential between two interest rates. Keen arbitrageurs are constantly on the lookout for this sort of opportunity.

Interest arbitrage

From another point of view the arbitrageur may start with a square book in both dollars and yen and then find that he is given six months' dollars on deposit at the bid rate of $8\frac{1}{16}$% per annum. At that time he cannot find a taker of dollars at anything better than that bid rate, but he does indentify a taker of six months' yen at the middle rate of $7\frac{3}{8}$% per annum. The 'round robin' in Table 2.4 sets up the forward quotation which has to be found to make the arbitrage work.

Table 2.4. 'Round robin' for a six months' covered interest arbitrage.

Transaction	Yen	Exchange ¥ per $	Transaction	US dollars
Spot purchase	210,000,000	210.00	Spot sale	1,000,000
Interest at $7\frac{3}{8}$% p.a.	7,743,750	(0.69)	Interest at $8\frac{1}{16}$% p.a.	40,312.50
Forward sale	217,743,750	209.31	Forward purchase	1,040,312.50

This swap margin of 0.69 yen per dollar is just six 'pips' (¥0.06) more by way of discount on the forward dollar than the ¥0.63 per dollar mentioned in the quotation. The ¥0.69 per dollar margin is thus the break-even point for this particular arbitrage. At this level there is no point in doing it for there is no improvement in the dollar yield of $8\frac{1}{16}$% per annum. However if it is possible to get any more 'pips' of discount in the forward margin the arbitrage becomes a possibility. Table 2.5 formulates the situation for a swap margin of ¥0.76 per dollar (the mid rate between the bid and the offer).

Table 2.5. 'Round robin' for a six months' covered interest arbitrage.

Transaction	Yen	Exchange ¥ per $	Transaction	US dollars
Spot purchase	210,000,000	210.00	Spot sale	1,000,000
Interest at $7\frac{3}{8}$% p.a.	7,743,750	(0.76)	Interest at $8\frac{1}{8}$% p.a.	40,641.13
Forward sale	217,743,750	209.24	Forward purchase	1,040,641.13

The dollar deposit taken at $8\frac{1}{16}$% per annum is thus enabled to earn $8\frac{1}{8}$% per annum, a betterment of $\frac{1}{16}$% per annum.

Any number of different examples can be postulated to show how the principles of interest arbitrage can be used in practical dealing operations. They all depend on finding suitable combinations of three variables: the two interest rates, and the forward exchange margin. Given the room within capital constraints to add money assets and liabilities to the balance sheet, interest arbitrage allows one to make markets for others by providing a forward exchange service between two countries.

If capital limitations, or local regulations, do constrain balance sheet growth, interest arbitrage can help to mitigate these strains. Assets acquired in one currency can then be funded with deposits accepted in another. This is particularly useful for a bank which has a developed deposit base in one

Arbitrage

currency, perhaps that of its home base, and assets in another. The economy in capital gearing or leverage is obvious. The same economy can be achieved by the outright sale of home base currency to supply the needed exchange into foreign currency. But the price for achieving capital economy by this means is the acceptance of an entirely unprotected exchange risk between the two currencies. A covered interest arbitrage obviates this risk and the requisite forward exchange contracts are 'off balance sheet'. As such the amount of capital cover required for them is only a fraction of that needed for 'on balance sheet' items.

Compounding

In banking the borrowing and lending of money is normally conducted on the basis of *simple* interest. The rate of interest may be fixed for the whole term of a contract, or it may vary at fixed intervals in accordance with changing interest rate levels. A 'floating' rate contract would typically call for the re-setting of the interest every six months on the basis of the then ruling market rate for six months' money. In any event the interest when due will be paid or accounted for separately from the principal amount of the underlying contract. It will not be added to it.

In *compounding*, however, the interest will be added to the original principal and not paid or accounted for separately. In such cases the interest rate is, for obvious reasons, always one that is fixed for the whole term of the contract. When this is so the 'round robin' formulation can readily be extended to cope with the mechanics. Table 2.6 sets out a simple compounding at the six months' point in a one year's deal using the data from Table 2.1.

Table 2.6. 'Round robin' for a year's interest arbitrage with one compounding.

Transaction	US dollars	Exchange ¥ per $	Transaction	Yen
Spot purchase	1,000,000	210.00	Spot sale	210,000,000
Interest at $8\frac{1}{8}$% p.a. for 6 months	40,625		Interest at $7\frac{3}{8}$% p.a. for 6 months	7,743,750
Principal at 6 months	1,040,625	(1.51)	Principal at 6 months	217,743,750
Interest at $8\frac{1}{8}$% p.a. for 6 months	42,275.30		Interest at $7\frac{3}{8}$% p.a. for 6 months	8,029,300
12 months' sale	1,082,900.30	208.49	12 months' purchase	225,773,150

The programming of a computer of adequate capacity to calculate a large number of compoundings of this type, one on top of the other, is straightforward. If each compounding is at an interval of, say, six months, a period of some years can be covered. But the effect of the compounding on the forward exchange margin needs to be considered. This is shown by comparison with Table 2.7 which sets out the same data as a straightforward one-year arbitrage without compounding.

Table 2.7. 'Round robin' for a year's interest arbitrage without compounding.

Transaction	US dollars	Exchange ¥ per $	Transaction	Yen
Spot purchase	1,000,000	210.00	Spot sale	210,000,000
Interest at $8\frac{1}{8}$% p.a.	81,250	(1.46)	Interest at $7\frac{3}{8}$% p.a.	15,487,500
12 months' sale	1,081,250	208.54	12 months' purchase	225,487,500

The effect of the compounding Table 2.6 is thus to increase the discount on the forward dollar against the yen at one year from ¥1.46 to ¥1.51. With an interest rate $\frac{3}{4}$% per annum higher than the yen the volume of dollars is inevitably growing faster than the yen volume. The effect of the compounding is to accelerate the rate of growth in dollar volume as compared with that in yen; and this becomes more marked with every successive compounding. The simple interest equivalents of the single compounding are 8.29% per annum for the dollars and 7.51% per annum for the yen. In numerical terms 8.290 is 0.165 greater than 8.125 which was the interest rate used for the dollars; 7.510 is only 0.135 greater than 7.375, the yen interest rate. The acceleration is revealed in the fact that whereas the increase from 8.125 to 8.290 is itself one of just over 2.0%, that from 7.375 to 7.510 is one of only 1.8%. The interest differential between the two currencies which had started at 0.75% per annum in terms of quoted rates has risen to the equivalent of 0.78% after only a single compounding. It will continue to increase, and at an increasing rate, after every successive compounding.

For the one year's arbitrage without compounding Table 2.7 deliberately used the same interest rate data as that in Table 2.1 and 2.5. This demonstrated the purely arithmetical effects of the single compounding. In practice a market does not often quote the *same* interest rate for a twelve months' period as that quoted for six months. Table 2.8 therefore sets out an uncompounded one-year arbitrage using the twelve months' interest rates which were quoted at the time when the rates of Table 2.1 were valid for six months' periods.

Table 2.8. 'Round robin' for a year's interest arbitrage (simple interest).

Transaction	US dollars	Exchange ¥ per $	Transaction	Yen
Spot purchase	1,000,000	210.00	Spot sale	210,000,000
Interest at $8\frac{3}{8}$% p.a.	83,750	(2.42)	Interest at $7\frac{1}{8}$% p.a.	14,962,500
12 months' sale	1,083,750	207.58	12 months' purchase	224,962,500

This is a totally different picture from that portrayed in Table 2.7. At the end of October 1985 the US dollar had a normally-shaped interest rate curve with the rate rising from $8\frac{1}{8}$% per annum at six months to $8\frac{3}{8}$% per annum at

Arbitrage

one year. By contrast the yen had an inverted curve with the rate falling from $7\frac{3}{8}\%$ per annum at six months to $7\frac{1}{8}\%$ per annum at one year. The interest rate differential of only $\frac{3}{4}\%$ per annum at six months increased to $1\frac{1}{4}\%$ at one year. Consequently a discount for forward dollars of only ¥0.76 for six months (as shown in Table 2.1) had become one of ¥2.42 for one year in Table 2.8. Over three times more discount was required for a one year's turn as compared with a six months' one.

Quotations in money and exchange markets are normally based on simple interest and the caution implicit in these examples is clear. The 'round robin' formulation will readily calculate interest rate arbitrages on a compound basis; but the resultant forward exchange margins will not necessarily correspond with those quoted in the market. It is by no means always possible to cover such exchange risks in interest arbitrages in the market. The difference between the dollar discount of ¥2.42 required in the market (Table 2.8) and the ¥1.51 projected in Table 2.6 is more than enough to destroy any arbitrage.

Open positions

A major requirement for successful interest arbitrage operations is the maintenance of an appropriate *open* position in each of the two currencies. This is essential to ensure exchange protection for both the interest that is to be paid in one currency and that which is to be received in the other. Moreover these open positions must be maintained for the whole term of the arbitrage.

The two simplest examples to consider are those formulated in the 'round robins' for straightforward six and twelve months' arbitrages shown in Tables 2.1 and 2.8. In Table 2.1 dollar interest is being earned; and its amount, namely US$40,625, is included in the dollar amount which is to be sold forward for delivery in six months' time. On the other hand, yen interest amounting to ¥7,743,750 is included in the amount of yen which has to be purchased for forward delivery at the end of the six months. In Table 2.8 the positions of the two currencies are the same way round but, as the arbitrage term extends for a whole year, the amounts are much larger. The six months' arbitrage requires an oversold open position of US$40,625 against an overbought position in yen of ¥7,743,750. The twelve months' example calls for a *short* position of US$83,750 against a *long* position in yen of ¥14,962,500.

Should any of these open positions be closed out, either wholly or in part, during the six or twelve months' terms the arbitrages are vitiated. The interest earned still has to be sold in exchange for that paid, but the assurance of so doing at the required exchange rates has been lost. Without this certainty the financial results of the arbitrages are themselves uncertain.

A simple example will make this clear, if we assume that, inadvertently or by design, the interest amounts in the one-year arbitrage are excluded from the forward cover. The exchange cover is then only partial, whereas in Table 2.8 it is complete. With interest excluded, only the principal amount of US$1 million would be swapped for one year against yen. Whilst, at the rates shown, this would still cost ¥210 million on the spot, it would produce only ¥207,580,000 in one year's time when the arbitrage is to end. At that time the dollar interest amounting to US$83,750 would still have to be sold and a total of ¥17,382,500 bought. The yen amount would have to cover both the ¥14,962,500 of yen interest payable *and* ¥2,420,000 of discount for the reduced value of the dollar in yen terms on the twelve months' forward contract.

If the spot exchange rate were, in a year's time, to have fallen to the ¥207.58 now quoted for twelve months' term then the US$83,750 would produce the full amount of yen which is needed. If the spot rate at the end of the arbitrage were any lower a loss would result; and were it higher there would be a windfall gain. Should the spot rate of ¥210 be at the same level in a year's time then US$83,750 would produce ¥17,587,500. On the other hand were the yen value of the dollar to fall over the year by *twice* the ¥2.42 discount shown in Table 2.8, the spot rate would be only ¥205.16 per dollar; US$83,750 would then produce only ¥17,182,150. As shown in the preceeding paragraph a total of ¥17,382,500 is needed. Thus a spot rate of ¥210 would lead to a windfall gain of ¥205,000; and a rate of ¥205.16 would produce a loss of ¥200,350.

The financial out-turn from the arbitrage is no longer certain. It is vitiated. The relatively small fluctuations postulated in this example for the yen rate over the year are only just over $1\frac{1}{8}\%$ in the rate itself. The windfall gain or loss is therefore relatively small. In the real world the yen/dollar rate has shown a much greater volatility than this. Recently the swing has been of the order of 16% in the rate. This volatility emphasises the risk that any windfall gains or losses could well be significant rather than trivial. On a fall of 20% from ¥210 the rate would become ¥168, at which level US$83,750 is worth only ¥14,070,000. That is a shortfall of ¥3,312,500 against the needed ¥17,382,500 and it entails the sale of a further US$19,717 to cover the yen shortfall. This is nearly 2% of the US$1 million principal.

Swapping

Swapping is essentially the writing of two separate exchange contracts at one and the same time. These contracts are in opposite directions and for different settlement dates. Under one contract currency A will be *purchased* in exchange for currency B for delivery on a specific date. Under the other contract currency A will be *sold* in exchange for currency B for delivery on a different date. In the foregoing interest arbitrage examples the first contract is shown as 'spot', that is for delivery under normal market conditions on the second working day after the date of the contract. It is this spot contract which actually moves the funds from one currency into the other. This contract clearly has to be executed in the spot foreign exchange market, and a suitable contract will be sought from the competing banks which provide a market for exchanges between the two designated currencies.

The second exchange contract in the interest arbitrage examples is shown as 'forward', that is for delivery in six or twelve months' time. It is this forward contract which guarantees the re-transfer back from currency A to currency B of the appropriate *amounts* on completion of the arbitrage. It is this contract which provides the protection for the arbitrage from the risk of an adverse movement in the exchange rate during its term. To achieve this the exchange rate governing the forward contract has to be fixed at the same time as that for the spot contract. This is the essential feature of a swap: both spot and forward rate are fixed at the same time. In nearly every case the spot and the forward rates will differ from each other. By fixing them at the same time the difference between the two is determined for the term of the arbitrage. It is this 'swap margin' which, as shown in the examples, is the key to the financial viability of the arbitrage.

Forward exchange cover is obtainable both in the inter-bank foreign exchange market along with the spot and, for some currencies, it is also available in traded markets for futures contracts. The principal markets are established on recognised exchanges in Chicago (Chicago Mercantile Exchange – CME) and London (London International Financial Futures Exchange – LIFFE), and the choice of possible markets is growing with the continuing development of futures trading in financial instruments. Inevitably, as with all such markets, the contracts themselves are standardised for amount, delivery and settlement. Furthermore the currencies for which such contracts are provided are limited in number to the few which are extensively traded around the world; and they have to be kept fully margined on a day-by-day basis against adverse movements in the currently quoted contract price. In principle the exchange rate cover needed for the forward contract in an interest arbitrage could be obtained by buying or selling futures contracts in a currency exchange. In fact this route is seldom followed chiefly because of the purely practical difficulty of achieving a sufficiently close match between the cover desired and that actually obtainable from the standardised contracts described above. Futures contracts are normally deliverable on only one working day in each calendar quarter and this is a major problem.

Consequently the forward exchange cover needed for an interest arbitrage is usually obtained from the inter-bank exchange market at the same time as the spot contract. Market-making banks can readily be found for 'spot against forward' swaps between most currencies; and the prices quoted are those of the swap margins themselves. After a trade has been concluded at a particular swap margin the spot rate to be used is adopted by mutual agreement. The forward rate is then determined by offsetting the swap margin against the spot rate.

This leaves the interest arbitrageur with only one problem. Foreign exchange swaps are normally traded for round amounts of one of the two currencies exchanged; and the same round amount will be used both on the spot and on the forward contract.

A spot purchase of US$1 million against yen on the spot would normally be counterbalanced in the swap with a sale of US$1 million against yen on the forward. But, for interest arbitrage purposes, the open position requirement described above means that the spot purchase and the forward sale are for *different* amounts. Table 2.8, for example, shows that, whilst

US$1 million has to be bought on the spot, US$1,083,750 has to be sold on the forward. To surmount this practical problem arbitrageurs tend to round up the larger amount that has to be traded, and then swap that. In the case of Table 2.8 a one-year swap might be written in the market for, say, US$1,100,000 as this is a reasonable rounding up for the forward amount which, as it includes the interest factor, is always the larger amount. A swap for US$1,100,000 would then produce US$100,000 more on the spot than was needed for the arbitrage. This unwanted US$100,000 would be squared off simply by selling it back into the spot market. The arbitrageur is then left with external contracts which amount to an unequal swap of US$1 million purchased on the spot against US$1,100,000 sold on the forward. The discrepancy in the interest arbitrage cover is then only US$16,250, the difference between the US$1,083,750 needed and the US$1,100,000 obtained. This additional oversold position of US$16,250 automatically becomes part of the arbitrageur's own overall open position and can be squared off with, or offset against, other 'retail' items of like dimension.

Management: control and accounting

Interest arbitrage dealing across currencies as described above presents some specific problems in the provision of the information needed both to manage the business successfully and to make sense of its financial results in profit and loss terms. The solution of these problems is the more essential in developed dealing rooms where interest arbitrage is a basic tool of the trade and where the dealing responsibilities are divided between several specialists, each possibly having his own team, and each concentrating on different markets within the ambit covered by the whole treasury function. A simple interest arbitrage of the type described will involve the money market traders in the two different currencies, the specialist swap dealer in the exchange, and quite possibly the spot dealer in the same exchange. Each one will need effective management information to enable him not merely to execute his part of the arbitrage but also to enable him to maintain, *vis-à-vis* the outside market, the open positions which are the key to the exercise.

On the financial front perhaps the chief problem lies in the differing and contrasting accounting conventions adopted by most accountants to determine the profit and loss results (a) of money market business and (b) of foreign exchange trading.

Moneys borrowed and lent are normally taken on to the balance sheet on an 'historic' basis. A US$1 million borrowed or lent will be posted as such. The normal profit and loss implications of the business are derived from the income and expense flows determined by the interest rates which are agreed as part of the borrowing or lending contracts. Interest payable or receivable is usually settled in cash either at the end of the contract or, for longer-term contracts, at specific intervals such as three or six months until maturity. Irrespective of interest settlement dates interest receivable and payable will normally be accounted for internally on an accrual basis over time. The interest amounts so accrued over each accounting period – and this is most frequently one month – are then fed into the profit and loss account for the period as either income or expense as appropriate. In the normal course of events no alterations are made in the balance sheet values of the underlying asset for money lent or liability for money borrowed. Where there are serious doubts about the continuing validity of the 'historic' values in the balance sheet, general or specific provisions may be made; but these will receive their own separate accounting treatment for profit and loss purposes.

By contrast the accounting convention applied to exchange trading is much simpler. The business is regarded as a straightforward commercial operation involving the buying and selling of various currencies. Each currency is treated as a separate 'product' in just the same way as a shopkeeper treats the separate lines in his stock. In each financial period purchases and sales are accounted for and the trading account opens and closes with valuations for the 'stock' or 'inventory'. For exchange trading this stock comprises the dealer's starting and finishing open positions. As the business is the exchange of one currency for another the dealer's open positions – unlike the shopkeeper's stock – will comprise both some positive ones, i.e. long positions and some negative ones, i.e. short positions.

From an interest arbitrage point of view the problem lies in the fluctuating basis on which 'open' foreign exchange positions are valued each time they are brought into the trading account at the end of a financial period. These closing open position values are then transmitted into the succeeding financial period as starting values. Open position values are thus one determinant of exchange trading profitability. Even if there has been no buying or selling of currencies during a financial period, that period will show a foreign exchange profit or loss if, at its close, a change is made in the valuation of the unchanged starting position.

The valuation of unchanged open positions held for foreign exchange trading fluctuates because, in vernacular terms, they are 'marked to market' before being brought into the trading account. This means that reference is made to the *external* inter-bank market in which foreign exchange quotations are made every time an internal financial period ends, and the then current rate is applied to each open position on the books. If the open position is a long one a profit will result if it is revalued as being worth more than before; it is a loss if its value declines. On the other hand a higher value will produce a loss on a short position, and a lower value a profit. Open positions may well include different classes of assets and liabilities each with its own distinct market values. In addition to spot (which usually includes contracts maturing within two days as well as money balances) there will almost certainly be forward exchange contracts and quite possibly futures contracts and foreign currency notes as well. In some foreign exchange systems these different classes of assets and liabilities are all revalued for profit and loss purposes at the spot rate. This is a further complication which simply introduces an element of irrationality in the profit and loss reporting of the underlying business.

The justification for revaluing at current rates those positions which are held for exchange trading is clear enough. The financial results for each trading period then stand on their own feet; and the closing positions are released into the next trading period at values commensurate with those at which they are currently being traded. But, as demonstrated above, interest arbitrage requires the maintenance of *external* open positions for the full term of each arbitrage. Fluctuations in the market values of these retained positions are irrelevant. As shown in every 'round robin', each arbitrage is fully protected against exchange fluctuations.

If *external* open positions held for arbitrage are, none the less, revalued during the term of the arbitrage (just as though they had been held for trading) this will not affect the overall result of the arbitrage (providing the positions are held); but it will distort the profit and loss flow over any intervening financial periods which end during the arbitrage. It will also inextricably mix up profits and losses on exchange trading proper with income and expense flows on interest account for an arbitrage. Given the high volatility of exchange rates in recent years the random profit and loss fluctuations induced by incorrectly applied revaluation procedures can be very worrisome. An external interest arbitrage position of US$1 million held throughout 1985 might, early in the year, have been valued in sterling terms at £952,380 when the rate was $1.05. Later in the year, when the rate touched US$1.50, it would have been revalued at only £666,667 – a fall of 30%.

Internal deals

Trading

As shown, it is essential for the successful conduct of interest arbitrage that the business be effectively controlled both in terms of the management information needed for the dealing operations themselves and to ensure that a proper accounting is made for it in profit and loss terms. Interest arbitrage is of such basic importance to the treasury business of most modern banks and business corporations that many practitioners now have interest arbitrage systems in place. They are heavily computer-dependent and all make use, to a greater or lesser degree, of the concept of the *internal deal*.

An internal deal is raised purely within the firm for each interest arbitrage that is set up. It records the details of each fully-covered interest arbitrage and is frequently set out in a format similar to the 'round robins' described here. In the first instance this enables the *mirror-image* of each position to be booked internally into the dealing positions of the traders concerned. Where different specialist traders or dealing teams are concerned with different aspects of an arbitrage the booking of the internal deal into the various sectors provides an effective co-ordinating mechanism for the activities of the separate specialists.

To go back to the first 'round robin' in Table 2.1 on page 17, an *internal* deal derived from it would present the various specialist dealers with the following *internal* positions:

1. The spot dollar/yen trader would be given a 'short' position of US$1 million and a countervailing 'long' position of ¥210 million. This would square off his trading book and ensure that he did not externally

Arbitrage

sell the US$1 million which had been purchased for the arbitrage until the *internal* deal was reversed at maturity.
2. The forward dollar/yen trader would receive similar information but in the reverse direction with a 'long' position of US$1,040,625 at six months against a 'short' position of ¥217,743,750.
3. The US dollar trader would receive a *liability* for six months' dollars thus obviating his need to square his book by taking in a deposit from the external market with which to fund the US$1 million which he had placed on account of the arbitrage.
4. Finally the yen trader would receive similar information but in the reverse direction with an *asset* of ¥210 million which would reflect the internal usage for the arbitrage of the yen funds which he had raised in the external market.

Traders are often encouraged, not simply to develop turnover in their specialities, but also to make markets in them by quoting each way dealing prices to acceptable counterparties. Such traders may get taken on either their bid or their offered side and will need to run positions akin to those of a stock exchange jobber in order to cope with their market-making activities. Where this is so it is perfectly feasible for interest arbitrages to be set up *internally* whereby the specialist market-making dealers take their portions of the arbitrage into their own trading books. In other words the *external* transactions required for an interest arbitrage do not necessarily have to take place *before* the internal deal is set up. If desired the internal deal can be set up first with some if not all of the internal positions which it creates being offset by later deals in the external markets at the discretion of the market-making specialists concerned.

Accounting

While internal deals cannot directly affect the results of dealings with the outside world they could clearly be used to transfer income or expense from one currency to another or from one function (such as foreign exchange) to another (such as money-market trading).

Effective control and supervision is thus essential for such deals and this is normally achieved by processing them through the accounting system and outside the control of the traders themselves. *Internal* deals are thus best processed almost exactly as though they were *external* ones where there is, or should be, a sharp divide between the traders who conduct the actual business and the operational and accounting staffs who process each individual transaction. Handled in this way internal deals are subject to the normal reviews by both internal and external auditors. An important element in these reviews is the monitoring of the exchange and interest rates used in the internal deals to ensure that they conform to those actually quoted in the relevant external markets at the time when the arbitrage was set up. Non-current rates are to be disallowed on internal deals just as much as on external ones.

The processing of dealing operations and their accounting tends to be labour intensive for both internal and external transactions; but modern computer installations can readily cope with all the processing required to account for internal interest arbitrage deals once the appropriate software programs have been adopted. There is a wide range of proprietary software packages available on the market for this particular function.

These programs all segregate the interest portions of the arbitrages and, by offsetting them against the forward transactions outstanding externally, they ensure that these elements (once they have been covered externally) are not included in the open positions which are subject to periodic re-valuation at fluctuating market prices. There is then no distortion in the exchange trading profit and loss derived from dealing turnover or open position taking. These interest elements are then amortised over the life of the arbitrage just as though they were interest flows (which in fact they are). By this means a true account is rendered on the usual accrual basis of the income and expense flows in the arbitrage for each of the financial periods during its life. If the six months' arbitrage shown in Table 2.1 on page 17 started at the beginning of a monthly profit and loss period then, at the end of the first month, the interest accruals from the internal deal would, save for the trading margin, offset those from the moneys lent and borrowed in the external market. Thus an expense would be internally accrued for one month's interest payable on the US$1 million placed externally under the arbitrage; and this expense would offset the income accrued for the one month's interest earned on the external asset. The contra accrual of an interest income would arise internally on the yen side of the arbitrage and, in profit and loss terms, this would offset the yen interest expense accrued in favour of the external depositor of the yen. Without these offsetting internal accruals the dollar side of the arbitrage would report nothing but the external interest income, and the yen side nothing but the external interest expense, throughout the term of the arbitrage.

Conclusion

Were the exchange and money markets 'perfect' in the sense in which this term is used by economists the windows of opportunity for the fully-covered interest arbitrages would be closed as soon as they were opened. Market-making specialists would quickly be closing up their quotations for money rates and exchange swaps and thereby eliminating the arbitrage opportunities. Interest arbitrage business would then be small beer with few participants bothering with it. The slender to nil margins implicit in the theoretical examples of 'round robins' set out in this chapter would discourage business.

In practice interest arbitrage is big business, and a basic technique which is extensively and continuously employed in all major dealing rooms; and this is not simply because it economises balance sheet footings as explained earlier. There is the more constructive side. Given access to viable money markets in two different currencies it is clear from the 'round robins' that a market-maker can construct a perfectly valid forward exchange market between the two currencies. Given access to the spot and forward exchange markets between two currencies plus a viable money market in one of them a market-maker can readily construct a viable 'offshore' money market for the other currency.

Interest arbitrage thus offers opportunities of expansion by the creation of new markets in response to the changing needs of the business community. Two recent examples of money-market creation come readily to mind. Some years ago, when international contracting firms entered Saudi Arabia to fulfil contracts for that country's infrastructure development, the need arose for a Saudi riyal money market to service their short-term requirements. At the time the riyal money market was relatively undeveloped within Saudi Arabia. None the less an 'offshore' riyal money market was constructed for the contractors by market-making banks using the riyal exchange market against the US dollar. The country's central bank provided the riyal/dollar exchange on the spot, commercial buyers and sellers of the riyal needed the forward cover, and the ubiquitous Eurodollar gave access to a highly liquid dollar money market.

More recently the rising prominence of the ECU (European Currency Unit) has demonstrated a much more generalised and widespread use of the techniques of interest arbitrage. There is now a large and widely used money market in ECUs which owes nothing to the direct support or intervention of any particular central bank. There is no central bank of issue for the ECU itself and, commercially speaking, it is best regarded as a packaged unit rather than a currency in the normal sense of the word. As a unit it comprises a finite amount of each of the currencies of the EEC countries; and the banks making the ECU market do have access to the domestic money and exchange markets in these countries. ECUs are thus assembled ('bundled' or 'packaged') in bulk by swapping appropriate amounts of the constituent currencies out of their original denomination against the US dollar. The dollar thus provides the basic exchange value for the ECU, just as it does for each of the constituent currencies, and the worldwide Eurodollar serves as the money market base. ECU interest rates are thus readily determined from the Eurodollar base as modulated by the swaps against each individual constituent currency. This is very big business indeed.

Finally, markets do in practice lack the degree of perfection needed instantly to close down the windows of opportunity for profitable interest arbitrage. Most active traders find it worth while to remain on the qui vive for profitable opportunities; and sometimes the window gets stuck ajar for a considerable period of time. Official statistics show that, for quite a while in 1985, banks in the United Kingdom were extensively moving funds out of sterling in exchange for foreign currency. Undoubtedly the apparent 'open' positions would have been covered by forward re-purchases of sterling and so the interest arbitrage framework is apparent. In their Monetary Bulletin of August 1985 the highly regarded monetary commentators at W. Greenwell & Co. estimated the volume of this particular interest arbitrage example to have been no less than £3.5 billion over the first seven months of the year. For such a high volume the countervalue must have been mainly in US dollars. Markets in other currencies would not have offered the scope.

Interest arbitrage

Thus at a time when foreign funds were flowing strongly into the United Kingdom for gilt-edged investment the banks, in selling sterling to foreigners, were provided with the opportunity themselves to arbitrage out of sterling and into dollars on a covered basis. The volume shows that this must have been well worth while and undoubtedly the banks would have been helped by the restraining control which the Bank of England exercised, for purely domestic reasons, over the interest rate structure in the sterling money market. Instead of immediately re-selling the dollars purchased from foreigners against sterling the banks could profitably retain them in dollar-denominated assets with forward cover against sterling. This window of opportunity for interest arbitrage was indeed well worth finding.

To take advantage of such opportunities market-making banks, and leading commercial firms too, have fully developed internal dealing systems on the lines described above. This furnishes the sophisticated control mechanism which is necessary for the effective management of fully-covered interest arbitrage. Internal deals provide practical co-ordination between specialist dealers, full processing which includes effective audit trails, and realistic accounting which distinguishes between those elements appropriate for profit and loss evaluation by revaluation and those, such as interest flows, for which the accrual or amortisation conventions are more suitable.

Note

Since writing this, the exchange rate for the dollar of ¥210 at the end of October 1985 has fallen to ¥155 at the end of July 1986; and this further 26% decline is not necessarily the end of the road.

Six months' interest rates have also fallen, but by 1% more for yen than for dollars. As the tabulation shows, the July 1986 dollar has thereby significantly increased its interest rate attractiveness over the yen for those, if any, who remain unconcerned at the exchange risk.

Six months' deposits	October 1985 % p.a.	July 1986 % p.a.	Change % p.a.
US dollar	$8\frac{1}{8}$	$6\frac{1}{2}$	$-1\frac{5}{8}$
Yen	$7\frac{3}{8}$	$4\frac{3}{4}$	$-2\frac{5}{8}$
Margin	$\frac{3}{4}$	$1\frac{3}{4}$	$+1$

CHAPTER 3

Securities arbitrage

Mungo Henderson and Ray Martine

Securities – instruments issued by properly constituted entities, typically sovereign states and bodies with limited liability incorporated under the laws of such states – have many of the characteristics of ordinary commerical contracts. The use of the term in its present meaning derives from the document held by a creditor as guarantee of payment and is first found in its modern sense around 1690. In the context of arbitrage, however, what perhaps particularly distinguishes securities is their longevity, amounting (from the point of view of an arbitrageur) to immortality. Although securities play an important role as collateral in the banking system they are, even more than money itself, vanishing as a physical species. The beautifully printed deed certifying that Josiah Smith was the proprietor of five debentures of One Hundred Pounds Each in the Buenos Aires and El Dorado Railway has been rendered almost extinct and certainly rendered obsolete by the computer entry (the 'street name'). While this has reduced almost to nothing one of the costs of classical arbitrage, it has equally gravely impaired one of the opportunities for profit.

This chapter seeks to draw its examples from a variety of ordinary or common shares and their derived and related instruments, and from the market in debt instruments, bonds. It is the authors' contention that the principles and opportunities are simple in concept, though infinitely variable in form.

It also touches very briefly on the long history of arbitrage in securities markets and on some modern practices and developments. It is however our clear conviction that while there will always be scope for the participant who will get up a little earlier in the morning, move a little faster and take telephone calls at even more disruptive hours, the true rewards in securities arbitrage will go to those who innovate and anticipate.

Historical background

Our present securities markets go back certainly to the seventeenth century, though Genoese and other capitalists were buying Spanish and Neapolitan bonds a hundred years earlier. Stock arbitrage as such probably dates from the development in both London and Amsterdam of flourishing markets in the securities issued by the British and Dutch governments to finance the wars against Louis XIV. However its major development came during the nineteenth-century booms, pre-eminently in government loans but also in railways, in the United States, in South America, in the East Indies and in South African gold mines which presented real, as well as spurious, opportunities to the holders of capital available for investment. Given the small size of capital markets in the period, the ability to access the major sources of finance, meaning at this time principally London and (at a considerable distance) New York and the European centres, could lead to a significant reduction in the cost of capital. The technological developments of the period gave an impetus to this process at least comparable to the communications revolution of today. The Rothschilds obtained news of Waterloo in 1815 by carrier pigeon. When Sir Robert Peel was appointed Prime Minister in 1834 he was in Rome; the journey to London took him the same 18 days it had taken the Emperor Hadrian nearly two millenia previously. Stock telegraphic services were introduced in 1867 by which time all major centres were linked by steam-powered ships and railway; and 20 years later they were able to communicate by telephone.

A nineteenth-century definition

The *Encyclopaedia Britannica* of 1875 has no doubts as to the importance of the subject:

'Arbitrage in stocks and shares is arbitrage properly so called, and so understood, whenever the word is mentioned without qualification among businessmen, and it is strictly a Stock Exchange business... defined to be a traffic consisting of the purchase (or sale) on one Stock Exchange and simultaneous or nearly simultaneous resale (or repurchase) on another... of the same amount in the same stocks or shares... at a difference in price sufficient to cover the cost of transmission, commission, interest and insurance, and leave an adequate profit... to be divided by the operators at both ends. The benefit to the various communities... consists – first... of... stability of prices of a large number of stocks and shares, and of an enormous amount of capital throughout the world; and second in the greater inducement... for the economy... in the use of capital, by means of a temporary investment in interest bearing securities with a minimized risk of fluctuation.'

A classic description of pure arbitrage. Yet to a world overshadowed by the US budget deficit requiring enormous flows of foreign capital and enlivened by the British government's privatisation programme, with huge volumes of British Petroleum, Britoil and British Telecom stock migrating between New York, the Continental centres and Tokyo on the one hand and London on the other, the 1875 description of the market has a familiar ring.

'The great government loans are, in the first instances, the natural subject matter of arbitrage: the new French Five percents, which with the United States Five Twenties cover in between them a round *£500 million sterling* probably stand first in the present list of arbitrage stocks. Indeed, but for the system of arbitrage it is not easy to see how the great French loans of 1871–72 could have been carried at all without convulsing the financial world. Arbitrage... by making the new security universally negotiable, enabled all the great bankers and capitalists of the world... to join... in concluding an operation gigantic even for modern times. Next to "French Fives" and US Five Twenties . . . come . . . ."Turkish", "Egyptian", "Italian", "Spanish", "Russian", some South American stocks . . . the shares and obligations of the great Lombardo-Venetian Railways . . . and . . . some East Indian securities.'

This environment – where over large and important parts of the world economy there were few or no controls on the movement of capital – was swept away in 1914, and even after the wholesale lifting of restrictions over the last dozen years it is still barely restored. However, within the controls which restricted capital movements there were, naturally, significant opportunities for profitable arbitrage, though their extent was by today's standards quite limited, and these furnished the background and the training from which today's arbitrage systems evolved, though perhaps without the constant innovation and experiment which characterises today's markets.

The investment dollar-pool and the sterling area

After the 1939–45 war, the British authorities found very high on their list of problems the constraints imposed by a shortage of foreign exchange, largely consequent upon the transformation of the United Kingdom from a major creditor nation to a substantial debtor. One of the natural consequences of this was the retention of the controls on capital movements brought in at the beginning of the war. The world was divided for this purpose into three zones.

1. The 'hard-dollar' zone: Canada and the United States and related economies
2. The 'sterling area': roughly the old Commonwealth and dependent territories excluding Canada
3. The 'soft-dollar' zone: the European countries and everywhere else.

Over time these separate entities merged, with the 'old sterling area' becoming foreign and so controlled in the era of currency traumas in 1968. With the suspension, though not the abolition, of exchange controls by the British Conservative government in 1979 this era ended and the United Kingdom rejoined the now rather limited number of sovereign states which permit domestic capital to move without restraint to seek the most attractive returns.

However, because typically the demand for the restricted 'pool' of external securities gave them a scarcity value, the investment dollar emerged in the active market in the artificial currency used to buy and sell these stocks. The investment dollar premium (the continuing excess value) reached the 60% level in the late 1960s when exchange rates were fixed and sterling clearly impossibly overvalued.

Primary markets

Historically, financial markets have repeatedly stood amazed at their own strength and skill and the prodigious feats they have performed in raising ever larger sums for their issuers. While discounting the more colourful metaphors and adjectives – but not the superlatives, which are usually justified – the utility of these operations is not in question. The cost of capital is lowered. By transforming local into global markets this effect is enhanced, broadening the range of participants and so lowering again the overall level of risk.

Aggressive marketing of primary issues in foreign markets has accordingly returned to favour in the last decade as capital has become again increasingly mobile and the incidence of saving in the national economies has become very uneven.

The prime example is the contribution made by long-term Japanese investors to the funding of the US government borrowings by the purchase of long-term obligations of the American Treasury. Also of considerable interest are the steps taken to ensure the successful placement of the equity shares of British Telecom, the formerly nationally owned telephone monopoly, which the Conservative government – for political as much as economic reasons – wished to see privatised.

Recent experience has shown that the most interesting results have been obtained by a careful analysis of the differing requirements of various classes of investor, typically as to risk preference, maturity requirement and perhaps above all tax status.

Classical arbitrage: an example

I am in London. De Beers are traded simultaneously in London, Paris and Johannesburg. My associate arbitrageurs in the other centres keep me in constant touch with their prices. It costs me one point to move De Beers stock from one centre to another and consummate purchase and sale with any counterparties there. The first price of the day is 202. Buyers emerge in Paris and bid up the price. I have the opportunity to buy in Johannesburg or London and sell in Paris. The amount I can obtain above 203 is a profit, to be divided among the arbitrageurs handling all aspects of the transaction after meeting their direct costs.

The classical case is based on an exogenous event to create an opportunity – buying or selling pressure in one centre – and requires the most rapid exchange of information, speedy execution of deals and the lowest, or at least competitive, costs.

Today's internationalisation of stock markets creates a huge number of opportunities which will be even greater in the emerging 24-hour markets, and the business of equalising the price of De Beers in all centres will remain the backbone of securities arbitrage even, or perhaps especially, in an electronically linked and visible market.

Opportunity creation

However, it has always been to creating, sometimes actually to fabricating, the conditions for the classical case that securities arbitrageurs have devoted their best efforts and where the extraordinary profits have been made.

The major and most immediate opportunities for successful (and unsuccessful) arbitrage lie not in moving securities between markets, but in the exchange of substitutes which carry a legal right to acquire or dispose of, and conversely an obligation to provide or accept, securities identical with an existing security on known terms and conditions. We list here the principal ones.

1. *Substitutable securities:* those considered to be interchangeable or having equivalent degrees of risk and opportunity.
2. *Convertible bonds:* debt instruments, convertible at a future date on known and certain terms, which may however vary with time, into the ordinary shares of a company.
3. *New shares:* issued by a company for a cash consideration, in a number of jurisdictions, particularly important in Britain, pro rata to the company's existing stockholders.
4. *Options:* to buy or sell shares on agreed terms at a future date. The market in options was revolutionised by the creation of the listed, traded option by the Chicago Exchange in the early 1970s.
5. *Futures:* on indices of a wide variety of securities.
6. *Obligations:* to deliver shares which trade as substitutes for the underlying security; notably *American Depositary Receipts*, issued by big New York houses against foreign securities (held for example by Morgan Guarantee) and traded in the American rather than the home market.
7. *Securities which separate and allocate differentially certain characteristics of an existing security:* notably Certificates of Accrual on Treasury Securities and similar issues.

1. *Substitutable securities*

The substitutable security was not invented by market operators. One of the largest corporations in the world provides huge possibilities for arbitrage in the stock prices of the holding companies for the empire created by the Englishman Samuels and the Dutchman, Deterling: Royal Dutch-Shell. This enormous enterprise is owned as to its equity, 60% by Royal Dutch Petroleum and 40% by Shell Transport and Trading, respectively Dutch and British corporations.

The following excerpt is taken from a review by Goldman Sachs in the summer of 1985:

'The 60/40 relationship.
The total market value of Royal Dutch should theoretically be 1½ times the total market value of Shell Transport. The basic "equalising" equation is derived as follows (where RD is the per share price of Royal Dutch, ST is the per share price of Shell, 268.0 million the number of Royal Dutch shares outstanding and 276.2 million the number of New York equivalent number of Shell outstanding) – (note one New York share equals four London shares. In London and in Shell Transport's balance sheet the company has 1004.8 million shares).

$$(268.0) \, RD = (1½) \times (276.2) \, ST$$
or
$$RD = 1.546 \, ST$$

At the present time, RD sells for $60.50 which implies a theoretical parity price for Shell of $39.13 (i.e. $60.50 divided by 1.546). This contrasts with Shell's current price of $37.75. Looked at another way, buying Shell Transport at $37.75 is equivalent to buying Royal Dutch at $58.28 (1.546 times $37.75).

From either viewpoint Shell is demonstrably cheaper than Royal Dutch. There is no substantive reason for this to be so. Dividend treatment for US investors is effectively the same for Shell and Royal Dutch. Thus US investors should be totally indifferent between owning Shell or Royal Dutch.

For some UK investors, the Shell dividend actually has the greater value (i.e. UK gross funds can recapture the withholding on the Shell dividend whereas Royal Dutch's dividend is subject to 15% Dutch withholding for these same investors and cannot be reclaimed). Thus this class of investors (that is the UK gross funds) should be willing to pay a slight premium for Shell.

In summary, new purchases should be directed at Shell rather than Royal Dutch (Shell is cheaper and yields more while underlying assets on both are identical). Aggressive investors should consider switching Royal Dutch to Shell as long as the current spread allows.'

Apart from certain minor effects of the differences between Dutch and British tax practice, investment in either identity is truly and completely equivalent. Clearly theory requires the relationship of the prices of the two stocks to deviate only marginally from the correct mathematical relationship. Historical accidents, however, in particular British Exchange control, have frequently caused the relationship to move quite arbitrarily and substantial disequilibrium to exist for prolonged periods of time. For a considerable period Shell Transport traded at a substantial premium to Royal Dutch because it was not open to British investors who held the bulk of the stock to acquire Royal Dutch without substantial present and future transactions costs, these being literally not susceptible of calculation.

Because of their extended lifespan and the widely differing objectives of their holders, securities can exhibit an ability to resist the basic rule of arbitrage which makes an ounce of gold sell at the same price in London and New York, less the costs of transmission and a margin of profit, and it is possible to observe instances where an anomalous relationship can exist for prolonged periods even though the instruments in question are transferable.

2. *Convertible bonds*

Typically a convertible bond is issued by a company using the incentive of an option to exchange into or subscribe for equity at a predetermined price and date to lower the rate of interest payable on the debt. If subsequent to the issue of the bonds the price of the related ordinary shares appreciates signficantly – premiums are typically quite modest on an investment-length view – the convertible will become a form of equity and will be arbitrageable against it. Prior to this, it will be possible to construct, using assumptions about money costs and the dividends on the underlying security, models giving equilibrium relationships which will indicate when divergences have created opportunites. However the normally modest size of convertible issues usually limits the opportunities. Recent developments in the Swiss franc convertible bond market, extensively used by Japanese companies,

Arbitrage

suggest that this is an area where as yet unexploited opportunities may present themselves.

In a recent case arbitrageurs were able to purchase convertible bonds of the Australian Bell Group which were due for conversion early in the New Year from the institution which had underwritten the issue in the first instance, but which wished to be clear of any involvement by its year end. While the bulk of the position was immediately covered by selling the appropriate number of Bell Group shares, a substantial holding, about 25% of the total, was not hedged but run as a high risk/high reward investment. Although overnight rates for Australian dollars were 22% over the two-week period that the position was held, the transaction proved extremely profitable.

3. *Issues of new shares*

In non-North American markets it is customary, and in many cases obligatory, for companies seeking fresh equity capital to offer to their existing shareholders the right to subscribe pro rata to their existing holdings. These 'rights' which carry the obligation as well as the right to subscribe are much more actively traded than is normal in the companies' stock. To ensure full subscription of the required monies it is customary to obtain commitments to purchase any shares not paid for – taken up – for a fee from the local institutions; a procedure known as underwriting.

This situation creates many possibilities for arbitrage because of the wide divergence of interests and abilities of the participants. Centrally, we find the existing stockholders of the company whom for this purpose we may divide into supporters, institutional investors, the general public and foreigners. The supporters/management/insiders will, almost by definition, have the clearest idea of the merits and purposes of the issue and the keenest desire and interest in its success and will accordingly be strongly concerned with this success; that is to say, its full subscription and a subsequent appreciation in the price of the stock. To this end as well as for corporate reasons they may be expected to respond in relatively predictable ways.

The institutional investor will be concerned on a variety of counts. He is a member of the underwriting syndicate and though he wishes to pick only the winners, knows that to a very considerable degree he has to take the rough with smooth. Underwriting commissions are a significant source of income to institutions. So in principle he will be happy to assume the obligation to take the stock if no one else will. This willingness will be compounded either positively or negatively by his existing position in the stock. Most major institutions hold a very large number of stocks and weight their portfolios to match more or less the structure of the market itself; at the extreme are programmed investment systems designed to match exactly the chosen indices.

Accordingly if a large company makes a rights issue, the investment or portfolio manager is confronted with a series of decisions:

1. Does he wish to increase his absolute commitment to XYZ in order to maintain his relative position?

2. Does he wish to increase his relative position – he must like the company somewhat or why is he holding it? If he does, the issue may – and often does – offer an opportunity to do so.
3. Does he have a significant cash flow which he is required to invest or an anticipated cash flow, say from interest or government bonds, paid twice yearly? This situation might be admirably addressed by the purchase in the market-place today – for a small amount, called the premium – of the right to pay the issuing company the larger amount, making it 'fully paid' called ('the call') and if the price declines significantly only the premium need be lost.

Unlike the institutional investor, whose main function is the prudent placement of fresh funds and new incremental savings, the general public (the private individual) is much more concerned with a fixed portfolio to which the addition of cash from outside is unusual. When confronted therefore by a request for additional capital from a company in which he already holds a position, his primary consideration is likely to be how to pay for it. And if he is a successful investor the liquidation of another holding could have unpleasant tax consequences which would make such a course irrational, whatever its theoretical merits. On balance therefore he will be a seller, even a forced seller.

Our last group, the foreign investors, is – not surprisingly – the one which can afford the most interesting opportunities. An extreme case is that of the beneficial owners of the stock backing the American Depositary Receipt. They are expressly debarred by United States law from taking up their entitlement, which must be sold in the market-place. The bulk of professional non-American investors are well placed to see that their interests are protected, but private individuals in distant markets often face considerable problems of notification and payment, even when the securities in question are held by professional custodians with a duty of care. On occasion payment dates can require the sale of entitlements without the beneficial owner having a say in the matter.

It is also open to companies to issue warrants or options convertible into equity at predetermined dates and prices. This practice has gained in popularity in some markets in a period of high interest rates as it can appear to create value almost out of thin air. On the one hand, if the price relationships are appropriate, the advantage or saving in interest, though not in purchasing, costs on the underlying ordinary share can be used to estimate a present value for the warrant or option, but on the other hand, typically stock prices are not usually correspondingly depressed by the potential dilution of earnings.

RTZ Company issues new shares at £2.00 each in the proportion of one new share for every five existing shares to shareholders of record on 30 September. There are 500 million shares in issue. The new issue will raise £200 million for the company.

Before the issue was announced RTZ shares traded at £5.00. The theoretical price of RTZ shares ex the issue will be equal to:

$$\frac{\text{the previous market capitalisation} + £200 \text{ million}}{\text{the increased number of shares in issue}}$$

$$\text{or } \frac{£2{,}500 \text{ million} + £200 \text{ million}}{£600 \text{ million}} = £4.50$$

with the new shares trading at a premium of £2.50.

In practice, large numbers of small parcels of new shares will come into the market and will be purchased by a very few institutional investors, quite probably acting with the sponsors to the issue and the company itself. In the example given, only a very large fall in the price of the stock would require the underwriters to meet even a part of their obligations. If however RTZ had chosen to raise an identical sum by issuing half the number of shares at twice the price, i.e. 50 million shares at £4.00, then a 10% drop in the stock price, a reasonable probability, could trigger such an event. The chances of price anomalies developing in such a situation are excellent. They are particularly good when foreign holdings are extensive.

In a recent issue by the Australian and New Zealand Bank, a security widely held by conservative investors in the United Kingdom, virtually the entire entitlement was repatriated to Australia. British investors were strongly influenced by fears of further currency depreciation and by the availability of attractive alternative investments in other securities, notably British bank shares, and disposed of their entitlements for a small premium, typically in small parcels. Arbitrageurs were able to build positions in the new nil paid shares, which were freely transmissible to Australia, and simultaneously were able to sell to that market fully paid shares for which there was a brisk institutional demand. The new shares furnished good delivery against the open shorts and the $1\frac{1}{2}$–2 point differential furnished a very satisfactory profit on the premium of 10–15 points, which was all the cash required, above the issue price of 375.

This opportunity arose as a result of the existence of a group of market participants with a particular bias: British investors called upon but reluctant to increase their commitment to an Australian Bank. An analagous but reversed situation arose in the conglomerate company North Broken Hill. In this case, because the stock was believed to be likely to be the target of an acquisition attempt by a corporate raider, new shares on which payments were due at subsequent dates were bid to a premium by speculative investors in Australia who used them, quite logically, as options with a declaration date equivalent to the date of payment on the call. It thus became possible to buy the old, fully paid shares in London and sell – at a premium greatly in excess of the carrying costs – the equivalent number of new nil paid shares in Australia. This exercise was enhanced by the payment of dividend to holders of the old shares, to which the new shares were not entitled. This differential was also disregarded by speculative investors looking for a major capital gain through the leverage which was available to them in the new shares.

By a pleasing irony, in this case the payment on the new shares was due in two instalments and after the payment of the first call, the Australian investors, – losing interest or hope – declined to bid the now partly-paid shares to be a premium. Becoming in their turn virtually forced sellers they drove the stock to a discount, enabling the arbitrage operation to be reversed.

4. *Options*

Before 1974, options were of limited relevance to securities arbitrageurs as the only options written were private contracts of the type now called London or European options.

The development of the listed option by the Chicago Board of Options in the mid 1970s completely transformed the situation. The principle, and to a much lesser degree the practice of trading securities options is now established worldwide. In the home country, the United States, the listed option some years ago obtained full recognition as a true 'security'.

The listed option, like the traditional option, is the right to buy or sell an exact quantity of a security at a predetermined price and date. Chicago's innovations were to standardise the options as to size, as to expiry date, as to right of exercise, and as to striking or exercise price and even more importantly by interposing a guarantor of substance, effectively the exchange itself, to eliminate the risk of non-performance.

By these steps its originators created an admirable market in risk which perfectly suits the arbitrageur. A Chicago option is a perfect substitute for the underlying stock but can be used quite differently. Crucial to this is the right of the holder of a Chicago option to convert at any time.

Although the uses of the option market are legion, we define here three categories of end-user. Pride of place must go to the straight buyer of an option contract who seeks to anticipate and profit from a move – a sharp move – in the underlying stock. He is buying leverage. At the other extreme lies the holder of a variety of stocks who wishes to hold this portfolio and to enhance the return on it by selling options. He will of course be prepared to sell both calls and puts as he is equally happy to sell stock he owns for a fee and to buy stock he would like to own even if the price has dropped – temporarily in his view – and even happier – though not necessarily correctly – to simply collect more and more fees. The third category wishes to limit his exposure to a market disaster – an interest rate hike, a revolution in Mexico – but yet retain a full interest in an upmove. Such an investor could obtain exactly this effect by holding the bulk (85%–80%) of his portfolio in cash and the balance in a portfolio of call options.

In all three cases what we have is a redistribution of risk, resulting in a proliferation of substitutable instruments. Central to all activity in this area is the problem of the valuation of options. Clearly, for a stock trading at 50, a three-month option is cheap at 0.5 and expensive at 5, but is there a central equilibrium price around which it should fluctuate? Securities markets have accepted and employ the models developed in Chicago by Black and Scholes to perform this function. Theory and experience confirm that the key variable is the volatility of the underlying security. Changes in volatility can create very choppy waters for the arbitrageur.

The use of options between centres can also be used to create significant profit opportunities. The Australian securities market is heavily weighted towards natural resource stocks. These companies have historically been favoured by overseas investors. As their products are traded and their prices fixed internationally, and their costs, or at least the bulk of their costs, are in Australian dollars, a devaluation of the Australian dollar will enhance their earnings and hence their value in Australian dollars. If such a devaluation were anticipated the portfolio investor would naturally purchase calls or Australian resource stocks, reasoning that his leverage to the stock price will more than compensate for the anticipated currency loss.

The option market provides very precise hedges which can be used to limit or eliminate the risk of loss in what would otherwise be a purely speculative position, which can also be very inexpensive and create the conditions that arbitrageurs require. Given the very wide variety of options available there are also opportunities in arbitraging between options.

5. *Stock futures*

The futures base their rationale on the rise of Modern Portfolio Theory and the resulting indexed funds. Modern Portfolio Theory argues that the evidence is that it is not realistic to expect portfolio management through stock selection to produce superior results. Historically it has failed to do so. In practice reliable results come from investing in the broad market. As the demand creates the supply so investment management groups designed for their clients portfolios which replicated whatever index was deemed appropriate for the purpose. Mathematical formulae determine the allocation of funds.

The market in Stock Index Futures and the options based on them dates from 1982 and there are many indices competing for attention. It does seem clear however that it will grow rapidly and increase in importance. Its protagonists claim that participation and response are markedly ahead of where the options market was at a comparable stage of its development. It is argued that the market in the main indices is, or will at least become, substantially more liquid than on the traditional exchanges. The market provides the normal advantages of a futures market to hedge commitments both foreseeable and postulated and can be used to hedge positions.

6. *American Depositary Receipts*

American Depositary Receipts (ADRs) are designed to enable US investors to hold and trade foreign securities in a convenient form. The size and depth of American markets is such that it is not unknown for the market in sizeable stocks to attempt to migrate to New York. The simple instance arises when investment demand for Matsushita Electric or Norsk Data, for British Petroleum or Vaal Reefs causes a significant proportion of the stock to be held and so traded in America. A related development is when, because of lower transaction costs rather than any market value discrepancy, it becomes cheaper for, say, a British investor to buy and sell BAT Industries or ICI in New York. Hitherto the most numerous companies with shares traded in ADR form have been South African gold mines and rather speculative Australian oil and mining companies. However, the extension of the system to a much wider range of stocks has potentially significant implications and could result in the opening up of a wider range of opportunities.

7. *Securities which separate and allocate differentially certain characteristics of an existing security*

Certificates of Accrual on Treasury Securities (CATS) the first of a whole menagerie of similar animals, were the brainchild of the New York house, Salomon Brothers. The objective was to market these separately to investors with particular tax and maturity preferences – there being in this case no risk of non-performance of the bond – by isolating certain of the characteristics found in a security issued by the United States Treasury, and so to enhance the value of the entire issue and create a profit opportunity through a pure though highly sophisticated arbitrage. The certificates in effect grant to one group of investors the stream of income from the underlying asset and to another the principal due at maturity. The appropriateness of these instruments to match very specific investment requirements raises their present value above the present value of the Treasury issue itself. While unquestionably a major and highly successful innovation in its market, it is worth comparing CATS to the investment trusts launched by a number of UK houses in the late 1960s which had capital and income shares with comparable claims on the trust's portfolio. These were usually equities, sometimes units in particular unit trusts; one trust concentrated on British government stock.

Currency conversion

Securities transactions can be used very effectively positioned against currencies. To use the Australian example, if a devaluation of the Australian dollar was anticipated the arbitrageur would purchase securities for Australian dollars in Australia and sell them into London or another market for another currency thus creating Australian dollar liabilities and non-Australian assets. This can be particularly interesting when the currency markets become difficult and expensive.

Acquisitions, take-overs and risk arbitrage

The offer by one company of its securities in exchange for those of another has always given rise to arbitrage opportunities, with the risk assumed varying in proportion to the probability of the success of the proposed mergers. Recent developments, primarily but by no means exclusively in the United States, have led to a widening of the role of the arbitrageurs or perhaps the meaning of the word itself. Arbitrage on Wall Street has come to mean essentially 'risk arbitrage': that is, the taking of positions in securities which it is judged – usually when one company has offered to acquire the stock of another, or in anticipation of such an offer – the arbitrageur will at a later date be able to set up a 'classic' arbitrage situation. It represents an extension of his role into those of analyst and money manager and calls for a very high degree of skill and sophistication. Because of the high degree of uncertainty involved in such situations the rewards have been very significant to participants prepared to accept the risks involved. To quote a notably successful practitioner, Ivan Boesky, 'an investor therefore must know all pertinent public information about the two companies involved'. It has been argued that arbitrageurs have moved along the road of innovation and creation to set up 'arbitrage' situations where none existed before by accumulating significant, and potentially controlling interests, with a view to creating a purchaser attracted, in the extreme instance, by the very existence of such blocks of stock. Along the way, large profits have been made by well-financed groups building up holdings on a basis of informed speculation for resale.

An example of this was the case of Gulf Oil. Gulf, a major American company, one of the original 'Seven Sisters', had in the opinion of many observers been indifferently managed for a number of years. Its appraised asset value was substantially in excess of the market price. A group of investors, headed by the chairman of a small oil company, Mesa Petroleum, built up a position in the stock and declared an intention to take steps to realise the underlying values for stockholders. As this declared policy developed, the Mesa Group contacted various oil companies to whom it promoted the idea – novel at the time – that so large a company might be acquired by purchase. Once mooted, this prospect proved so attractive that there was no shortage of interested parties, and a large expansion in the number of 'arbitrageurs', Wall Street style, prepared to position in Gulf stock. This build-up in the number of shares explicitly designed to be sold on played a considerable role in bringing pressure to bear on the Gulf management who after considerable efforts to retain control of the company in which their stockholdings were insignificant, established a 'friendly' buyer for Gulf, Chevron, at a price not too different from the original Mesa target and which gave very substantial profits to stockholders and arbitrageurs who had been prepared to assume the inherent risk.

A classic example is provided by the history of MLC Ltd, the holding company for The Mutual Life and Citizens Assurance Co. Ltd, Australia's third largest life insurance company and one of only two quoted investment vehicles in this field in that country.

For some years MLC had been very poorly managed, despite its wide operating base, very large portfolio and opportunities. Moves to increase control by the British Sun Alliance Group, holders of 20% of the equity, were blocked by the Australian regulatory authorities. The construction and property group Lend Lease established a signficant holding, following pressure from institutional investors for managerial improvements. At this stage the New Zealand Group, Industrial Equity, judging that there was little downside risk and substantial upside potential, became aggressive buyers of the stock and built up a holding of just under 20% of MLC's equity, the level beyond which under Australian securities law, restrictive provisions apply. The Lend Lease group did the same.

Subsequently, Lend Lease made a partial bid for 49% of MLC and was able by a share exchange scheme to raise its holding to 69%. It then bid for the balance of the shares. Industrial Equity accepted ultimately a bid specially designed to minimise its tax liability. Acceptance was at $28 per MLC share against a book cost of $3.20 or a multiple of 7.7 times the investment.

Settlement

Securities markets operate a wide variety of settlement periods around two different settlement systems. The systems are either cash settlement, typified by New York, or account settlement, most notably in London.

In a cash settlement system, payment is due in cash on a given day after the transaction (five working days in New York). An account system however permits bargains within the account period to be offset against each other so that a purchase of 1,000 ICI and a matching sale of 1,000, if effected within the period, will excuse the purchaser from putting up the purchase price in cash. He remains of course liable for or entitled to the difference on the trades. Additionally the London settlement is not effected on the last day of the account but ten days later, normally on the second Tuesday after the second Friday in the two-week account. A seller on the first day of the account will therefore not be entitled to payment for a day over three weeks. The seller of the same security under the cash settlement system will be in quite a different position. This position has been eroded by the increase in bargains for Cash Against Delivery and centralised clearing but remains functionally intact. Differences naturally arise in the process of settlement. These have been known on occasion to destroy the profitability of an operation, particularly when management has not invested in the necessary systems and personnel. We would wish to lay the greatest stress on the importance of such an investment, the more so because observation suggests that there is often a reluctance in the securities industry to use personnel with the necessary ability and qualifications on grounds of cost.

In large part these problems are being addressed or submerged in the creation of large centralised clearing systems, Cedel and Euroclear, and the American Depositary Receipt system. As, however, markets become more closely linked – and in the short term at least this trend looks more likely to accelerate than to reverse – we look for the straightforward transmission of a parcel of stock from London to Hong Kong – the consummation of the classical arbitrage – to be replaced as the crucial activity by the conversion of one security into its equivalent (the exercise of options, the payment of calls, subscription monies) in the primary market where the participants are different.

The new world

In our judgement the profitability has gone from true simultaneous arbitrage. An element of risk must now be assumed in all arbitrage-type securities transactions. This risk and the extent of potential losses need to be the subject of rigorous analysis. That said, the rewards to the innovating and the skilful can be substantial.

CHAPTER 4

Commodity trading in different currencies

Alex McClumpha

Dealers in soft commodities have always been strongly aware of the currency dimension in their operations. However, only in the last 20 years has there been developed a skill and expertise in foreign currency trading amongst their customers and other users of soft commodity markets. Growing volatility in exchange rates since the collapse of the Bretton Woods monetary agreement and the need to work in an environment without fixed points of reference, caused both brokers and dealers, as well as the users of soft commodities, to re-evaluate the use and relevance of futures markets in general.

The 1970s saw a great increase in dissemination of information about the futures market concept and the interest taken in using existing markets by speculative and investment houses, especially under the stimulus of the first oil price shock in 1973 and the international inflation that followed. In the complex of factors which go to make up the spot and the forward prices available at any minute during the opening hours of the world soft commodity exchanges trading floors, currency rates have become in recent years the most readily available explanation for short-term market price movement, particularly when there was no other discernible change in the fundamental market factors influencing the commodity. Currency change has also become the most widely accepted reason given for all price volatility, not otherwise apparent.

It is arguable whether this increased consciousness of exchange rate movements has been a result of more intrinsic volatility in soft commodity futures markets, or mainly of the change in world economic conditions since the dramatic rise in oil prices. Another reason could be the increased publicity and sophistication attaching to the financial markets. To establish the importance of currency influences in the major soft commodity markets, it is necessary to examine the basis on which this type of trading is carried on.

Definition of soft commodity markets

The description 'soft commodity markets' is used for futures markets, excluding those trading in metals or financial futures. These are markets for international commodities, usually of tropical origin, such as cocoa, coffee and sugar, which comprise the main London-based soft commodity markets. In recent years the term has been extended to those markets organised on the London Commodity Exchange, including rubber. It could be expected that the cereal and grain markets, especially soya, would be included in this description; but for other reasons it is usual to regard these markets as a separate group.

Third World governments receive benefit from direct food aid, subsidised exports and trade agreements, in a wide variety. Exchange rates rarely have any consumer impact but these are fixed by the importing country government which will normally control the issue of import licences.

There is a fundamental difference in trade organisation and the influence of currency factors on a commodity which is principally imported by the countries of Africa and Latin America, and one which is largely produced and sold by those countries.

For these reasons our definition of soft commodity markets will be limited to those which are international in trading; that is, with a range of producing and consuming countries and where futures markets exist in more than one of the world's major trading centres. This limits the description of the importance of currency considerations, and especially the conclusions to be drawn and the examples to be used, to the major world soft commodities of cocoa, coffee and sugar. Futures markets exist for these internationally traded, largely tropically produced commodities, in both New York and London, traditionally the trading axis of the world, although there are minor markets in both Paris and Amsterdam.

The development of trading in futures

All these markets owe their origins to the uncertainties of doing business in the import and export of the physical commodity. In the last century insurance was sought for the contractual consequences of the failure of goods to arrive by the due date, or against the potential loss of a vessel. Expectations of delivery achievement or failure gave rise to the creation of the futures market in which the trader could hedge his risk. The use of this market changed with the growth of modern communications to give more emphasis to changes in the conditions of supply and demand; the risk of crop failures became more readily apparent with the development of forecasting methods in agriculture; while the green revolution has come from the increase in knowledge of agricultural techniques and the investment possibilities in agricultural production. On the consumption side modern marketing techniques coupled with the development of processing facilities in the consuming countries have expanded demand and allowed consumption to absorb increases in production. Perhaps more significantly for the activities of the market-place, the development of predictive market research has improved the ability of the futures market to consider fundamental supply and demand factors well into the future.

In the period up to the 1970s, the commodity markets were concerned to provide an opportunity for dealers to hedge their risks, and the markets worked at a relatively low level of purely speculative activity. London and

Arbitrage

New York commodity arbitrage helped to achieve an economic distribution of supply in line with demand. Most users of the commodity, particularly in Europe, confined futures activity to routine hedging and many preferred to deal only in the physical commodity, leaving the more sophisticated application of futures market techniques to the professional.

The oil price shocks (1971–73 and 1975–77)

The tremendous upheaval in world economic conditions resulting from the OPEC-inspired oil price increase, beginning in 1971 and reaching its climax in 1973, had a considerable effect upon all commodity markets. More business users saw the importance of linking their commodity activities with their foreign exchange transactions at the contract rather than at the delivery stage. It became apparent that the connection between a physical contract in dollars and a position on the relevant London market in sterling had to be managed.

The general rise in commodity prices, and especially the huge amounts of dollars earned by the oil producers in seeking profitable investment, began to produce a considerable revolution in soft commodity markets.

1. Raw materials price increases forced a wide range of major industries to pay close attention to their procurement policies. This included the analysis of risk, in some cases leading to increased use of futures markets, close examination of stock levels, and forward planning and commitments, and – for the first time for many years – concern about maintaining overall growth against the background of higher output prices and increasing inflation. Futures markets received much unaccustomed publicity, sometimes as a means of insuring against unrestrained cost increases, but perhaps more often as apparent contributors to uncontrolled cost increases. Whatever the reason, the springboard for the growth of the futures industry was put into place.
2. There was a rapid increase in the funds available for investment in futures markets. An excess of dollars in the hand of the oil producers spilled over into commodity investment funds, in turn developing with a volatile and inflating set of world commodity prices. It became commonplace that commodities could provide a general hedge against inflation.
3. During this period also there was a rapid growth in the sophisticated communications industry. Market intelligence became instantaneously available in a new telecommunications development worldwide. It also saw the growth of the computer funds with advanced charting and investment management techniques. As the futures industry came of age, all the techniques adopted and refined by the soft commodities markets followed the best practice available in any futures market and were encouraged by the continued growth in business and market price volatility. At this time market professionals were very conscious of being in an industry with dramatic growth.

Against this background of interrelationship of function, regardless of the actual commodity traded, soft commodity markets developed an awareness of the impact of world financial and economic conditions on their commodities which were very different from those of the past. Now world conditions were able to remove funds from one market to another not because of fundamental supply and demand factors but simply because the prospect of price volatility might be greater in an area unrelated to soft commodities. The size of the funds invested in commodity markets was reaching such a proportion that the purely trade business was dominated to the extreme that chart trading was able to control market price movements to the exclusion of the fundamental supply and demand factors for considerable periods of time.

Marketing

The soft commodity markets seem to attract business in several ways. Some are directed towards providing an efficient facility for the handling of investment funds. This relates to the ability of a market to show volatility and good volume and to be free of excessive charges and margin requirements as well as giving confidence to the investor of efficient systems in an environment reasonably free of government regulation or other forms of control that may impinge on the ability of the international trader to take profits or move funds readily from one area of the world to another or from one market to another. It goes without saying that an attractive market to the international investor must be located in a currency and in a part of the world where that investor has confidence.

Customer needs

The users of the commodity market who are producers, consumers or dealers in the commodity concerned also require the above facilities, although they may need to operate in a less than perfect market, if there is no better alternative. Only a few years ago it was enough that the commodity market provided a routine hedging facility. However, one of the problems caused by the surge of investment funds into commodities has been a shift in the major influences. Weight of investment is now as important as supply and demand as a short-term price determinant. The scale of investment has been so large at times in soft commodities that the fundamental factors and the traditional dealers and market operators have been submerged in waves of investment money. This has raised the danger of the market becoming unrepresentative of the situation in the commodity and thus unattractive to the commodity customer, not least because hedges may well result in huge margin calls, sometimes totally out of scale with the underlying business. In a situation such as this currency cover takes on additional importance.

Today's hedging market is also called upon to provide cover against a political risk. This may be civil unrest of one type or another such as the virtual civil war that interrupted the flow of coffee from Uganda for many months. Physical contracts may also be annulled by government action or similar forms of uninsurable risk. It is difficult to envisage any effective hedge against this sort of development but the soft commodity

Producer needs

markets are called upon to provide for the eventuality, however imperfectly. Normal commercial risks in the physical commodity supply chain require a reliable hedge.

Producer needs

Tropical commodity producers have no long-term history of using commodity futures markets, although theoretically they are available and provide an attractive facility. Central Marketing Board, government agency operations and a general political distrust of consumer-dominated marketing facilities have characterised producer activities in commodities. The political preference has been for international co-operation through the various international commodity agreements to assure as near as possible fixed returns to the producing countries.

Marketability

Up to 1976 the belief that commodity markets provided the only effective hedge against inflation and currency depreciation was widespread, especially after gold had been revealed as an ultimately poor hedge, owing to the unwillingness of the traditional holders to continue to invest in the metal. It was widely believed, as the world recovered from the second oil shock, that the resurgence of economic activity would again justify substantial long holding of soft commodities. The reality was different.

Economies and efficiencies in industry worldwide had resulted in more effective use of minimum stock levels, and the end of the period of sustained economic growth led to uncertainties and even continued recession in many industries, so that forward commitments were kept to a minimum. Holders of physical commodities began to have concern for their ability to find a market for their commitments. Gradually prices came under pressure with the volume of forward trading falling substantially. Today commodity users are less inclined to make forward purchases because of economic uncertainty and are willing to accept short-term risk at high price levels rather than enter into long-term commitments.

Producers have rarely felt comfortable in selling far forward. So at present the soft commodity markets, in spite of considerable volatility in the nearby positions, are very thin in the forward positions. The risk of being forced to finance an unsold physical position in a major commodity is not readily accepted in today's markets. Conversely, the willingness of the users to trade and to undo and reinstate hedges and to utilise arbitrage opportunities is greater than before. The liquidity provided by this activity can still attract investment funds but on a selective basis.

Pricing soft commodities

The process of price formation in the soft commodity markets is achieved by open outcry bidding until a traded price level is agreed. A fundamental characteristic of these markets is that there is always a buyer and always a seller under certain conditions of price. Market price at any moment therefore includes an implicit analysis of the fundamental supply and demand factors, crop estimates, anticipated consumption, weather conditions, shipping conditions, and any other political and economic factors that could conceivably affect the commodity concerned including forward currency rates.

It is not an objective calculation, but simply a synthesis of market views, including proximity of chart points and other technical factors. While it is usual to explain the market movement by reference to a particular event or a rumour, the reality is more complex. Currency movements, for example, are rarely significant for the market as a whole. They will be swallowed in the economic or political factors involved in an active physical market. Similarly, currency movements will affect price levels in London or New York or Paris, at the same time but in different directions, usually with no net effect on the average international price of the commodity.

It is usual for soft commodity market prices to be initially established in US dollars. London prices and those quoted in other centres after allowing for contract differences will be the local currency price converted at ruling exchange rates.

Spot prices

Much attention is paid to the terms of the delivery contract in all commodity markets. Each contract must, in theory, be able to be fulfilled by a delivery of the physical commodity, of known quality and under very specific terms. From time to time local conditions such as delayed shipments, or deliberate market manipulation may allow the effective divorce of the spot price from the forward price. Under normal circumstances, if spot prices in London and New York appear to be out of line then the market will adjust by moving the physical commodity in whichever direction is necessary to balance the distribution. This implies that the price in one market will be sufficient to allow the trade a margin after having paid the cost of shipping and bringing the commodity to account in the other market. However, if time does not allow this process to take place before the expiry of the contract that may be commanding a premium, short-term price relationships between spot and forward can be broken and the divergence will only be bridged between buyer and seller in the premium market-place regardless of market or currency fundamentals.

Normally arbitrage adjustments between London and New York will prevent such an abnormal situation occurring, but when the time available for correction by physical movement is too short such special conditions can occur.

Forward prices

Forward prices include the currency element but this is inevitably subordinate to the fundamentals of the commodity. In effect, commodity factors could result in the market quoting forward prices at a discount, where the currency market demands forward premiums. This factor alone makes the soft commodity market a difficult vehicle for straightforward currency hedging. The structure of the forward price is not achieved by any means that would reveal an exact correlation with forward currencies. At best it offers the market participant the opportunity to hedge his currency risk or to open a currency risk at the same time as he hedges his raw material costs, but not the opportunity to separate the risks as he could by making separate currency transactions. The idea of hedging a currency risk in a forward commodity futures market simply implies a disproportionate risk in the commodity to which the currency risk will always be subordinate.

The only exception to this could have been in the case of possible currency devaluation before the general adoption of floating rates. Economic theory could have predicted the direction an expected devaluation would have had on the London/New York commodity market price spreads. The process of selling London and buying New York cocoa, for example, would have yielded currency profits at the time of the 1967 sterling devaluation, but this is not really relevant experience to either the commodity market or the currency market in 1986.

Although a forward currency risk may show an opposite trend to the commodity risk, it will nevertheless reflect forward interest rates and will not therefore constitute a separate risk to the commodity trader who will usually be content to arrange his finance and utilise a single hedge. A speculative market participant, however, will see the currency risk differently and would need to consider separate foreign exchange cover in dealing in a commodity market designated in another currency.

Arbitrage opportunities

In the forward positions, where traded volume is usually heaviest between two and six months forward, arbitrage considerations include a number of elements. For example, the situation outlined in Table 4.1 was to be found in the cocoa market during March 1986.

Table 4.1. The cocoa market, March 1986.

Position	London £ per tonne	New York $ per tonne	Exchange rate $ per £
May	1,540 ($2,242)	2,070	1.456
July	1,565 ($2,266)	2,100	1.448
May arbitrage + $172			
July arbitrage + $166			

The simple indication to sell London and buy New York is, however, not an adequate response. Unlike financial markets, commodity markets need to reflect the physical commodity. In this case, it is necessary to take account of the following factors in the evaluation:

1. Freight and delivery costs between European tender ports from the London contract and New York. Such costs vary within a small range and amount to between $130 and $150 per tonne.

2. Quality differentials are also an important arbitrage variable. During the above period, Ivory Coast cocoa traded at May London basis minus £35 ($51) and at May New York basis plus £20 ($29) as the New York market usually reflects Brazilian-origin cocoa.
3. Other variable elements include interest rate differences, commissions and other financing costs.

It can be seen from this that the impact of the quality differential is more important than the freight cost.

However, to the holder of Ivory Coast cocoa in Europe the evaluation might appear as follows:

Sell $ equivalent of May London per tonne	2,242
Buy May New York	2,070
Arbitrage	+172
Compared with the physical market:	
Sell Ivory Coast cocoa for May London	2,242
Less quality differential	51
	2,191
Buy Ivory Coast cocoa in New York	2,070
Plus quality premium	29
Plus freight cost to Europe	130
	2,229
Physical loss	− 38

In the absence of other market factors the London price may be expected to fall relative to New York towards the equivalent of $2,229 but only if European physical demand for Ivory Coast coffee improves will the quality differential reduce.

Similarly, the New York price should rise but the level reflects the availability of Brazilian cocoa which dominates the New York markets.

Holders of other origins of physical cocoa will have different evaluations, so that the would-be arbitrageur needs a knowledge of the physical cocoa market supply conditions to evaluate the arbitrage premium and its probable direction of movement.

The cocoa quality arbitrage premium is not fixed, except in the short term. In the above example, a two-cent variation in the exchange rate would affect the arbitrage calculation by about $38 per tonne. If there are no short-term movements in cocoa differentials then a movement of this magnitude may result in short-term relative market price corrections of benefit to the arbitrageur.

London–New York arbitrage of this type allows advantage to be taken of currency change in the short term with protection against overall market movement by holding a long position in one market against a short position in the other. The risk in other than the short term is that the cocoa differentials will change and it is this sort of arbitrage that offers large potential benefits for the cocoa trader, but risk for the currency arbitrageur.

Differentials are principally affected by the following:

1. Supply from origin, both physical availability and political involvement in marketing.
2. Demand for certain types of cocoa relative to particular supply.
3. Shipping and other logistical considerations.
4. Large positions held against futures markets.

It is not unusual for differentials for a particular origin of cocoa to swing from a minus of £30 to a premium of £250 over the appropriate futures month in London.

For hedgers, the choice of market in which to take a position is often governed by the type of cocoa involved and also by the currency of payment for the physical transaction. However, for the short-term currency arbitrageur there may be enough stability of differentials in the short term to allow useful benefits.

It is probable that exchange rate influences are slower to affect commodity markets than purely financial markets and it is certain that the commodity trader will consider his arbitrage activities on a longer time scale than the short-term speculator.

Arbitrage dangers

The influence of the physical market is always paramount in commodity market analysis.

For the currency trader the impact of the physical market and his risk is least:

1. in the short term: that is, within the spot market position where physical commodity movement is limited by lack of time for adjustment (although it should be remembered that this could lead either to relative stability, where supply is assured, or to exaggerated local price movement where there is a significant short or long market position, tightly held);
2. where the market is constrained by excess supply, including the impact of commodity agreements, as in coffee.

In any period of slack, currency movements can provide the basis for effective arbitrage positions and the commodity traders will also tend to operate on these movements.

The danger of physical movement swamping the size and altering the direction of a currency arbitrage appears when:

1. supply interference occurs – this can be purely logistical or more difficult to handle where particular qualities are affected, as when a government decides to withhold supplies for political reasons;
2. market operators secure the medium-term market based on expectations that differ markedly from currency trends.

Recent trends in the world coffee market illustrate these dangers for an arbitrageur. Under the influence of an international commodity agreement and a more than adequate world supply, the London futures market based upon robusta coffee and the New York market based upon mild coffees established a fairly stable premium in New York of about 30 cents per lb over London. This was reflected in the physical market also. Arbitrage between the two markets was routine and often provided price movement simply because of currency changes. In October 1985 the realisation of drought in Brazil caused dramatic change in coffee supply, and market prices began to reflect the new situation (Table 4.2).

Table 4.2. The coffee market, October 1985 and March 1986.

May position	London £ per tonne	$ per lb equivalent	New York $ per lb	Arbitrage cents	Exchange rate $ per £
October 1985	1,736	1.099	1.474	+ 37.5	1.396
March 1986	2,560	1.691	2.496	+ 80.6	1.456
Change		+ 0.592	+ 1.022	+ 43.1	0.060

It is evident that differential price change between the two markets, within the overall price rise, changed dramatically boosting the New York premium by 43.1 cents. Over the same period currency moves were in the opposite direction. Any arbitrage depending upon currency would have been swamped, even though it was correctly based.

Disaster can speedily overtake the currency arbitrageur operating in a commodity market with this sort of behaviour.

Further caution is necessary in rapidly moving markets. Rules for most New York markets call for a limit to daily price movement. For example in coffee, trading is not permitted beyond a 6 cents per lb limit per day. This can result in traders being prevented from establishing or liquidating a position while prices are rising or falling strongly. At times early in 1986 the coffee market was unavailable for the best part of four days, while the London market continued without limit, resulting in a huge shift in the arbitrage which could not be covered for a considerable time.

Hedging

The soft commodity markets are well designed to provide for the hedger in international trade. This effectively limits the traditional hedge to a volume of the commodity actually traded in dollars, sterling and, to a degree, French francs. Both cocoa and coffee and, to a lesser extent, sugar, are produced in countries of the Third World all of whom are affected by the problems of international debt and usually heavy domestic inflation or at least detailed governmental control over international payments. Cocoa produced in Ghana is bought from the farmer by government agencies, paying in Ghana cedis. Although Ghana sells cocoa to the international market in dollars, there is no contact and no contract between the farmer and the international market. Sales in dollars by Ghana can be hedged by both buyer and seller in the cocoa market against market movements, but the European buyer will need to take his currency hedge separately unless the final currency in which chocolate is to be sold is sterling, in which case the currency hedge will be included in the London/New York cocoa market arbitrage.

It follows that although as previously stated there would be a disproportionate risk in hedging the currency risk alone by using commodity futures, the reverse is not the case. Many holders of cocoa contracts in sterling or in dollars may well seek to cover the currency risk for their final sales in Deutschmarks or lire separately. This type of cover would have the added advantage of allowing separation of the currency risk premium from the commodity risk premium as well as settlement on a different time scale if required. A separation of the currency cover from the commodity cover simplifies the analysis of the separate risks and allows for a different response to the conditions ruling in each market as well as a more sensitive risk management in general. A user who required regular supplies of coffee, for example, might also be a net receiver of dollars elsewhere in the business and might choose to open his currency risk while at the same time securing a forward position in coffee.

For a British company purchases of coffee in the London coffee futures market automatically provide cover for any currency risk assuming the end product of the transaction will be the sale of coffee to the consumer in the United Kingdom. However, there may be advantage in not allowing the currency risk against a physical contract in dollars to close, if currency relationships at the time of the coffee futures contract are judged to be unfavourable. Today the existence of effective currency markets allows this risk to be kept open whilst maintaining the option to close the currency contract separately from the commodities futures transaction. Certainly there will be times when a currency transaction seen as part of the hedging of the commodity is out of line with the currency hedge obtainable in currency futures markets or directly from inter-bank sources. Separation of these two risks provides a useful facility.

The concept of currency risk in commodity futures is less familiar in the United States. Today, even where the United States is by no means the largest consumer in the world, nearly all commodities are traded in dollars. This is certainly true of the soft commodities with organised commodities futures markets. As a result the majority of consumers outside the United States are used to the existence of a currency risk forming part of their commodities exposure and the practice of considering this risk separately from the commodity risk alone is well understood. It is, however, only recently that much effort has been made to attempt more active management of a currency risk.

Currency risk coverage

Handling the currency risk in soft commodities can be done in a number of ways. For a user of the commodity the prime concern is always the cost of the commodity against the view of the market and the potential cost impact on his business into the future. In general the acquisition of physical supply governed by crop conditions, logistics and producer marketing activities will be regarded as the most difficult part of the transaction. As a result most dealers and users will obtain physical supplies whenever they are available and seek to adjust the timing of the pricing process by futures market operation.

If overall expectations are for a market decline in a commodity the conclusion of the physical contract might be matched by a prior sale of futures or by the conclusion of a physical contract on price-fixing terms related to the market. With the physical purchase normally in dollars an exchange risk exposure is created which can be:

1. covered immediately;
2. left until spot purchase is necessary to satisfy the payment terms of the physical contract;
3. covered at some intermediate time.

Forward cover of the exchange risk can be got in a futures market or through the banks' foreign exchange facilities. There may be a practical advantage in using the financial futures market if it is intended to trade actively in the currency. However, it is more usual for commodity market operators to fix their currency cover and to concentrate their active trading on the commodity market where price movements are usually more significant.

Similarly if overall market expectation is for a market price increase, the users will seek to buy futures contracts and will be encouraged to do so by the probable scarcity of physical commodity offerings. Futures contracts acquired in this way will be sold as physical supplies gradually become available. In this case even with futures contracts denominated in sterling the currency risk is unlikely to be seen as significant or separate from the commodity price development. It is not routine for holders of the more distant forward commodity futures contracts to automatically cover the currency. Commodity markets and currency markets operate on slightly different time scales and the commodity operator may well tend to defer his currency cover until it falls within the three- to six-month range and then perhaps to delay until a favourable moment for action is seen.

Increasingly commodity trading organisations will manage their currency exposure as a portfolio and put less emphasis on taking specific cover for particular physical or futures contracts. There is overall today a greater willingness to increase the velocity of trading and to arbitrage in both soft commodity markets and in currencies. This trend will probably increase as commodity futures markets themselves develop their scope even further.

The commodity risk will continue to outweigh the currency risk but the availability of futures facilities leads to the increased use of arbitrage, both currency based for short-term operations or to enhance activity in a static market. Short-term arbitrage is particularly useful to improve a hedge position on a quality-based arbitrage, but must be seen as a subsidiary activity which is always liable to be offset by events in the commodity itself.

CHAPTER 5

Financial futures

Brian Larkman

Development of the financial futures markets

Of the many developments which have changed the shape of the world's financial markets in recent times, few have had such a far reaching impact as the introduction of trading in financial futures contracts. The collapse of the Bretton Woods and Smithsonian agreements in the early 1970s presaged an era of unprecedented volatility in interest and exchange rates which created a need for new instruments which could be used to manage the increased risks which resulted. Given their vast experience of the economic benefits of futures contracts in the agricultural industry, it was not altogether surprising that the two major Chicago futures exchanges, the Chicago Board of Trade (CBT) and the Chicago Mercantile Exchange (CME), should respond to this challenge by extending their activities into the financial sector.

Financial futures trading began on 16 May 1972 with the introduction of seven currency contracts on the newly formed International Monetary Market (IMM), a division of the CME. By current standards, the early progress of these contracts was sedate but as time progressed the concept of financial futures trading gained more widespread acceptance and in 1975 attention turned to interest rate futures with the introduction of a contract based on GNMA (Government National Mortgage Association) collateralised depositary receipts on the CBT. Early in 1976 the IMM introduced a contract based on 90-day US Treasury Bills and this very successful contract was followed over the next five years by contracts based on US Treasury Bonds and Notes on the CBT and three-month Eurodollars and domestic CDs (bank certificates of deposit) on the IMM. Partly because of policy changes adopted by the US Federal Reserve Board in October 1979, this was a period of rapid growth in financial futures trading during which many other contracts were introduced by other US exchanges. For a number of reasons, however, few of these contracts enjoyed the success of their Chicago counterparts and many were delisted within a relatively short space of time.

The industry took another major step forward, however, in April 1982 with the introduction of the first Stock Index contract – based on the Standard and Poor's 500 Index – on the IMM, and later that year the London International Financial Futures Exchange (LIFFE) became the first fully-fledged financial futures market in the European time zone when its doors opened for business on 30 September. Within six months LIFFE was trading three interest rate contracts based on short-term Eurodollar and domestic sterling time deposits and long-term gilts together with four IMM-style currency contracts, each of which is quoted against the US dollar. Since then, LIFFE has introduced its own Stock Index contract, based on the Financial Times Stock Exchange 100 Index, and further interest rate contracts based on long-term US Treasury Bonds and short-dated gilts.

In recent years the internationalisation of financial futures trading has progressed at a remarkable pace. After two years of careful preparation, the Singapore International Monetary Exchange (SIMEX) opened for business on 5 September 1984 incorporating an innovative link with the IMM by means of which positions initiated on one exchange can be closed out by offsetting trades transacted on the other. This 'mutual offset' arrangement has considerable attractions for many multinational organisations which now use futures to manage risk on a worldwide basis and in spite of the considerable technical and regulatory problems which have to be overcome, it seems likely that further links between other exchanges will be developed along similar lines over the coming years.

Alongside the developments we have already mentioned, the economic relevance of financial futures trading has gained acceptance in a number of other financial centres in Europe and the Far East. On 19 October 1985, the Tokyo Stock Exchange introduced a contract based on long-term domestic Japanese yen bonds which was greeted with enormous enthusiasm. Unfortunately, a few days later the Bank of Japan announced its intention to allow interest rates to rise in order to promote the appreciation of the yen/US dollar exchange rate and the subsequent collapse of the Japanese bond market had serious consequences for many small investors who had been encouraged to support the new futures instrument. Even so, there are many who see tremendous long-term potential in this contract and the eve of trading in Tokyo saw the respective chairmen of the CBT and LIFFE signing a memorandum of intent to develop an identical contract on each exchange as the first step towards the creation of a 24-hour market in Japanese bond futures.

Even now, plans for the introduction of financial futures in Paris and Zurich are well advanced and the Sydney Futures Exchange is expected to commence trading in Eurodollar futures some time during 1986 – a development which may well involve a direct linkage with LIFFE. Meanwhile, ECU (European Currency Unit) futures commenced trading on FINEX (a division of the New York Cotton Exchange) on 7 January 1986 and on the IMM eight days later.

Undoubtedly, the sheer pace of the financial futures revolution has prompted concern among the industry's leaders and regulators and many doubt the ability of traders, brokers and customers alike to cope with the bewildering array of instruments now available to them. Nevertheless, the industry has flourished, largely as a result of its ability to respond quickly and effectively to changing trends in the market place, and, given the fiercely competitive environment which exists within and between the exchanges mentioned, there is little sign that its rapid rate of development is likely to abate for some time to come.

Features of trading

Formally, a futures contract is a legally binding agreement between two parties under which one party agrees to make, and the other to take delivery of a given quantity and quality of a particular commodity on a predetermined date or range of dates in the future at a price which is fixed at the time the contract is made. This concept is simple enough to understand when applied to futures contracts on physical commodities such as soya beans, corn or copper and it can be translated into financial terms most easily by regarding money – in its various forms – simply as a commodity in its own right.

There are several important features of financial futures contracts, and the way they are traded, which distinguish them clearly from other types of forward trading. Firstly, financial futures are highly standardised contracts which are traded by open outcry on centralised and regulated exchanges. Generally, each exchange designates a specific area of its trading floor – known as a pit – to each contract, and all bargains are struck between members standing within the confines of the pit concerned during clearly defined trading hours. Theoretically, this is almost an ideal method of trading in that there is only one price for each commodity at any given time and that price is available to all parties who have an interest in the contract at that moment. By means of modern telecommunications systems this price information is disseminated almost instantaneously to offices and dealing rooms around the world. The corollary of these arrangements, however, is that at peak times, and on the announcement of any unexpected news, trading in the pits can become frantic and with obligations relating to many millions of dollars or pounds changing hands in a matter of seconds, very detailed and comprehensive regulations must be rigorously applied by exchange officials to ensure an orderly market and the responsible execution of clients' business.

The second important distinction between futures trading and other forward markets concerns the manner in which settlement and delivery arrangements are made. Although the details vary between markets, essentially each futures exchange is supported by a centralised clearing house which effectively assumes the role of the counterparty in each transaction and thereby guarantees the performance of each contract traded. By becoming the buyer to every seller and the seller to every buyer, the clearing house always has a balanced position but, even so, it is only able to provide the financial guarantee mentioned for two reasons:

1. Every transaction must be registered in the name of a clearing member whose standing is acceptable to the clearing house.
2. In respect of every contract which is left open overnight, the clearing house requires the clearing member concerned to post an initial margin deposit in cash or some other form of acceptable security.

The level of initial margin required, which may vary from time to time in the light of changing market conditions, represents a small percentage of the face value of the contract concerned, providing the futures trader with a high leverage effect on the cash resources he has available. In the second phase of this margining process, each contract which remains open overnight is revalued by reference to the official closing price in the market and, generally, all profits and losses resulting from this 'marking to market' process are available for distribution, or have to be made good, in cash on a daily basis. This daily cash flow is termed 'variation margin'.

In this way the clearing house ensures that its maximum risk in respect of any contract outstanding is limited to the amount of unpaid margin monies due. This can be carefully controlled and, if necessary, the clearing house reserves the right to close out positions in order to protect its position. These formal rules on initial and variation margin arrangements exist only between each clearing house and its clearing members, but the rules of most exchanges normally insist that arrangements made between clearing members and their clients should ensure the prompt payment of margins on terms which are at least as strict as those applied by the clearing house itself.

The third area in which the clearing house plays a vital role is in connection with the delivery and settlement of futures contracts which have not previously been closed out by offsetting transactions in the market. In practice, only a small percentage of futures transactions results in physical delivery of the underlying instrument but the delivery process is an integral part of the specification of each contract and provides the mechanism by which convergence between cash and futures prices is assured. All exchanges determine a given sequence of contract months – usually based on a March, June, September, December quarterly cycle – and specify that delivery should take place either on one day in each of these months or on any day of the month at the option of one of the parties – usually the short – to each transaction.

However, in recent times the need for such formal delivery arrangements has diminished, particularly following the enormously successful introduction of Stock Index futures, and in the interests of simplicity a number of contracts have been designed without the facility for physical delivery to take place. The settlement of these contracts if they are allowed to run to maturity is made in cash which simply means the payment of variation margin up to the final settlement price at the close of trading on the last trading day. In the design of these contracts, of course, great care is taken to ensure that the exchange delivery settlement price (EDSP) is exactly in line with cash market prices at the time in question and that there is no scope for the manipulation of these prices by large-scale professional operators.

The tendency on most US exchanges has been for the clearing house to be owned by the clearing members of the exchange concerned but, in contrast, LIFFE has chosen to clear through the International Commodities Clearing House Ltd, an independent clearing company which is owned by the major UK clearing banks and thus is financially independent of the exchanges it serves.

The nature of the contracts available

At this point we are ready to consider in more detail some of the important characteristics of those contracts with which we will be involved later in the chapter. Highlights from the specifications of these contracts can be found in Appendix 2 (pages 86–87). However, any trader who is seeking to pursue arbitrage opportunities through the use of these instruments is advised to study carefully the detailed specification of each contract as defined by the exchange concerned, as a thorough understanding of the terms of each contract is essential for successful arbitrage trading.

Broadly speaking, the contracts which interest us fall into three categories:

Short-term interest rate futures

Table 5.1. Short-term interest rate futures.

Contract	Exchange(s)	Value	Maturity
Eurodollars	IMM, LIFFE, SIMEX	$1,000,000	3 months
Short sterling	LIFFE	£500,000	3 months

For the purpose of this analysis, we will not dwell on the US Treasury Bill and CD contracts trading on the IMM. Although these instruments also track short-term interest rates, in recent times they have lost liquidity while the Eurodollar contract has emerged as the pre-eminent short-term futures instrument reflecting the enormous depth of the inter-bank market from which it is derived.

Prices of all short-term interest rate futures are quoted on the basis of an index which is calculated by subtracting from 100 the annual interest rate on the instrument concerned. These prices move in increments of 0.01% (termed one basis point) and the cash value associated with such a price change is $25 for the US dollar-denominated contracts and £12.50 for the LIFFE short sterling contract.

It is important to recognise, however, that the time deposit contracts mentioned are not based upon deposits which are already in existence at the time each futures deal is struck. Rather, the purchase of a futures contract represents an obligation to create a three-month cash deposit on the relevant delivery date if the futures position is held until then. This point has important implications for the pricing of these contracts as we shall see later.

In practice, although LIFFE initially constructed a somewhat cumbersome delivery mechanism for these instruments in order to satisfy certain legal considerations, only a handful of physical deliveries ever took place on this basis. In September 1984 the specification of these contracts was simplified by removing the physical delivery mechanism completely as a result of which all maturing long and short positions are now settled for cash in the manner described above.

Futures on long-term fixed coupon securities

Table 5.2. Long-term fixed interest futures.

Contract	Exchange(s)	Nominal value	Coupon	Maturity of deliverables
US Treasury bond	CBT, LIFFE	$100,000	8%	15 years or more
Long gilt	LIFFE	£50,000	12%	15–25 years

The design of this set of futures contracts is more in keeping with traditional commodity market arrangements in that for each contract there is defined a set of cash market instruments which can be delivered into a maturing short futures position. Each futures instrument is based upon a notional bond or gilt (with coupons of 8% and 12% respectively) to which the various deliverable instruments trading in the cash market are related by a system of price factors. These price factors, which are defined by the exchange concerned, compensate for differences in coupons and maturities and are applied to the exchange delivery settlement price of the futures contract to determine the invoice amount which is payable by the holder of a maturing long position for the bonds or gilts allocated to him under the delivery process.

In keeping with convention in the cash market, price quotations are for $100 or £100 nominal of each instrument and prices move in increments of $\frac{1}{32}$nd. Having regard for the relative sizes of the contracts mentioned above, the cash value associated with a price movement of this size is either $31.25 or £15.625.

Currency futures

Table 5.3. Currency futures.

Contract*	Exchange(s)	Value
Sterling	IMM	£25,000
Deutschmarks	and	DM125,000
Swiss francs	LIFFE	SF125,000
Japanese yen		¥12,500,000

*There are various other less active currency futures on the IMM.

Essentially, currency futures are directly analogous to highly standardised forward contracts in the currencies concerned. Each is quoted against the US dollar and, in keeping with commodity market practice – unlike the foreign exchange market – all price quotations reflect the dollar value of one unit of currency. Thus a dollar/Deutschmark exchange rate of 2.50 translates into a futures market price of 0.4000 and the maxim 'buy low – sell high' can be applied consistently across this whole range of instruments.

Generally, prices move in increments of 0.05 cents, creating a tick value of $12.50, but an exception to this rule is the LIFFE sterling currency contract for which the tick size has been reduced to 0.01 cents ($2.50) in the interests of promoting trading activity.

63

Arbitrage

In each instance, the maturity of outstanding futures contracts results in physical delivery of the currencies concerned in the principal financial centres of the countries involved, with settlement being made through the relevant clearing house system.

Basic cash/futures relationships

At any given time, the price at which a futures contract trades is a complex function of the forces of supply and demand which are applied by a wide variety of hedgers and traders whose interests are motivated by a multitude of different factors. It would be naive to presume, however, that the combination of all these influences results in a price which represents no more than the market's perception of the future spot price of the commodity or financial instrument concerned. Such a conclusion ignores the role of arbitrage in the markets and at the heart of these arbitrage activities lie the basic relationships which link the various financial futures contracts we have described to the cash market instruments from which they are derived. In the context of this volume we are unable to undertake a rigorous theoretical analysis of the generalised commodity model but the essential features involved can be demonstrated clearly enough by examination of the practical application of this theory to the three groups of futures contracts we have introduced. Let us consider each in turn.

Short-term interest rate futures

In many respects the short-term interest rate futures created by the IMM and LIFFE on the basis of inter-bank time deposit facilities are unusual in the sense that the underlying cash market instruments cannot be bought for cash and delivered into a futures contract when it matures. As a result, it is not possible to relate futures prices to current interest rates by considering the cost of carry because this concept cannot readily be defined.

However, by simultaneously borrowing and lending in the cash market for different maturities it is possible to fix in advance interest rates for periods of time in the future – termed forward/forward rates – and as this process is directly analogous to the purchase or sale of appropriate futures contracts, the interest rates which can be secured by these means should be broadly equivalent to each other.

The construction of a forward/forward lending rate is depicted in Fig. 5.1.

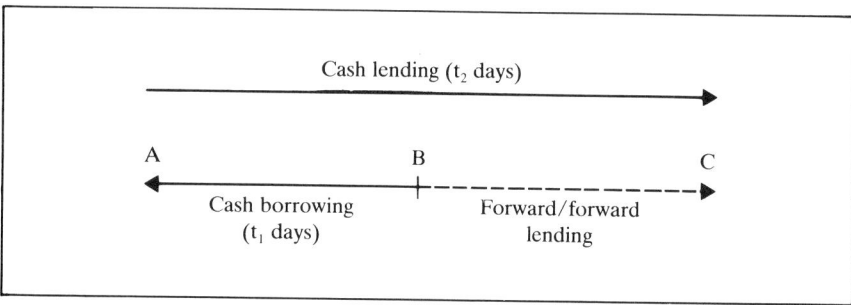

Fig. 5.1. Construction of a forward/forward lending rate.

Financial futures

In order to fix in advance the interest rate he will receive on a lending over the period BC, a bank dealer can borrow the funds he requires from the market over period AB and simultaneously lend them over the extended period AC. Let us assume that the lending is made for t_2 days at $r_2\%$ and the borrowing is taken for t_1 days at $r_1\%$. If r_{ff} represents the forward/forward lending rate so created, then (on the basis of a 360-day year)

$$(1 + \frac{r_1 t_1}{36,000})(1 + \frac{r_{ff}(t_2 - t_1)}{36,000}) = 1 + \frac{r_2 t_2}{36,000}$$

and $r_{ff} =$

$$\left[\frac{1 + \frac{r_2 t_2}{36,000}}{1 + \frac{r_1 t_1}{36,000}} - 1\right] \times \frac{36,000}{(t_2 - t_1)}$$

or, alternatively,

$$r_{ff} = \frac{r_2 t_2 - r_1 t_1}{(t_2 - t_1) \cdot (1 + \frac{r_1 t_1}{36,000})}$$

The derivation of a forward/forward borrowing rate, created by borrowing over the longer period t_2 and lending over the shorter period t_1, is calculated in an exactly similar way although it will be appreciated that a different result will be obtained when account is taken of the bid-offer spread in the cash market for each of the transactions involved.

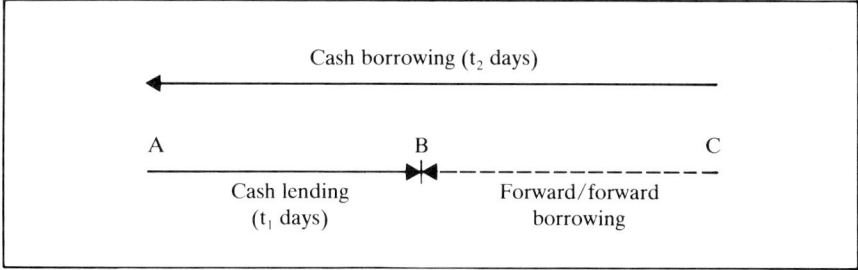

Fig. 5.2. Construction of a forward/forward borrowing rate.

Calculations of this nature can be applied to any combination of mismatched loans and deposits with maturities up to one year. For longer periods the calculations are not so straightforward as allowance must be made for the settlement of interest on the anniversary of each transaction before it reaches maturity. This point acquires particular significance when one of the transactions is over, and the other under, 12 months' duration in which case a closed form solution is not obtainable and the result will depend on the reinvestment rate received on interest paid before maturity.

Now we know that within certain limits the sale of a Eurodollar or short sterling futures contract fixes the offer rate for a three months' borrowing which starts on the delivery date of the contract concerned. Provided the period covered by the futures contract is identical to the gap created by the cash market transactions mentioned above, the interest rates implied by these alternative approaches to the same problem should be in line with each other.

As an illustration of the manner in which these techniques are applied in practice, Table 5.4 has been computed from data drawn from the Eurodollar inter-bank and futures markets on 19 December 1985 (for settlement on 23 December 1985).

Table 5.4. Comparison of theoretical and actual Eurodollar futures prices.

Futures delivery date	Days	Cash rates (%)	Implied fwd/fwd prices	Actual LIFFE future price
19 Mar 1986	86	$8\frac{1}{16}-7\frac{15}{16}$	91.97–92.33	92.23
18 Jun 1986	177	$8\frac{1}{16}-7\frac{15}{16}$	92.01–92.60	92.14
17 Sep 1986	268	$8\frac{1}{16}-7\frac{15}{16}$	91.81–92.63	91.92
17 Dec 1986	359	$8\frac{1}{8}-8$	91.73–92.77	91.64
	(450	$8\frac{3}{16}-8\frac{1}{16}$)		

Several important conclusions can be drawn from this table. The most obvious point to make is that the first three futures contracts, at least, lie within the ranges predicted by the cash market yield curve. Additionally, as the three month Eurodollar futures contract tracks the offer side of the market, it could be argued that the prices of the first three futures contract months are marginally higher than expected. From a hedging viewpoint this may suggest that, of the two alternative methods described for fixing borrowing rates for the periods involved, the futures route appears preferable. On the other hand, the price of the December 1986 futures contract appears unusually low but it does not follow that this represents a viable arbitrage opportunity because of the costs involved in exploiting the modest discrepancy identified. We will say more on this subject later.

Equally interesting is the fact that the spread between the bid and offered forward/forward rates widens progressively (by some 22/23 basis points for each three-month period) owing to the impact of the time factor on the bid-offer spread in the cash market. From this we can deduce that there is a considerable range over which the prices of remote futures contracts can move before they appear to be out of line with the cash market. As a corollary, however, it is reasonable to suppose that these same remote contracts are likely to offer the greatest arbitrage potential to a trader who is able to operate on favourable terms in the cash market. Certainly this has been borne out by experience of the Eurodollar futures market since trading began four years ago.

Futures on medium- and long-term fixed coupon securities

The relationship between longer-term fixed coupon securities and their futures derivatives follows more closely the classic model for physical commodities as – subject to certain conditions – these instruments can be carried and may be delivered into successive futures contracts.

With such securities it is possible to fix in advance the price at which a given bond or gilt may be sold by selling short an appropriate number of futures contracts. It follows that if the markets are at all efficient, the difference between the current cash price of any deliverable US Treasury Bond or UK gilt and the current price of a related futures contract (adjusted to allow for differences in coupon and maturity) should reflect, quite simply, the cost of carry during the period until the futures contract matures. In a positive yield curve environment, this carry will also be positive and the adjusted price of the futures contract will lie below current cash market prices whilst futures prices will become greater than equivalent cash market prices when the yield curve assumes a negative slope.

This straightforward analysis can be rearranged without difficulty to derive the short-term financing rate implicit in a combination of cash and futures prices for a given bond or stock. In equilibrium, this implied repo rate, as it is called, should be in line with current short-term interest rates in the market and, if this is not the case, an arbitrage opportunity may exist.

In its simplest form, the cash and carry result can be expressed

$$\text{Profit/Loss} = [\text{factorised futures price} \times 500] + \text{accrued interest} - \text{interest costs} - \text{cash purchase price}$$

and when the markets are in equilibrium, the result of this calculation should be very close to zero. In practice, a detailed formula for evaluating this relationship is complex as it must take into account exact coupon payment dates and assumed reinvestment rates, taxes, commissions and the cost of funding initial and variation margins. However, a close approximation will be given by the following expression:

$$\text{Profit/Loss} = \left[GF \times PF + \frac{ct_0}{365} \right] + \sum_i \frac{c}{2}\left(1 + \frac{r_1 t_1}{365}\right)$$
$$- \left[GC \cdot \left(1 + \frac{r_2 t_2}{365}\right) \times 500 \right]$$
$$- \left[PF \times 1000 \times \frac{r_2 t_2}{365} \right]$$

where GF, GC and PF represent the futures and cash dealing prices and price factor respectively and c is the coupon on the gilt acquired; r_1 and r_2 are assumed reinvestment and borrowing rates; and t_0, t_1 and t_2 represent in turn the number of days accrued interest in the gilt at delivery, the number of days for which any coupon received is held until delivery and the number of days of carry of the arbitrage.

By way of illustration, Table 5.5 has been computed on this basis from data extracted from the markets on 19 December 1985 at a time when the Mar 86 LIFFE long gilt contract was trading at a price of $110\frac{23}{32}$nds. Although these calculations are not exact, they demonstrate clearly the wide variety of results which is obtained by applying the standard 'cash and carry' operations mentioned above to each of the cash market gilts involved. What is evident from this analysis is that there is one gilt which maximises the return on this type of transaction: the $11\frac{1}{2}\%$ Treasury Stock 2001/04. By definition, the seller of each futures contract which is held until maturity can select which of

Table 5.5. Comparison of long gilt cash and futures prices.

Stock	Clean cash price £	Price factor*	Factorised futures price £	Carry (incl. margin costs)	Profit/Loss per £50,000 nominal
10% Conversion 2002	95.875	0.8592	95.130	−0.3280	−£536
11½% Treasury 2001/04	106.351	0.9636	106.689	−0.3010	+£18
12½% Treasury 2003/05	114.654	1.0364	114.749	−0.2541	−£80
8% Treasury 2002/06	81.143	0.6972	77.193	−0.3698	−£2,160
11¾% Treasury 2003/7	108.841	0.9812	108.637	−0.2175	−£211
13½% Treasury 2004/08	122.995	1.1101	122.909	−0.3030	−£195
5½% Treasury 2008/12	59.871	0.4830	53.477	−0.3587	−£3,376

* The exact LIFFE price factors have been rounded to the fourth decimal place.

the eligible gilts he wishes to deliver into his short position and the presumption is that he will choose that stock which offers him the highest return in a 'cash and carry' operation. Hence, this stock is termed the 'cheapest deliverable' and is the stock whose price movements will be tracked by the futures market. It should be noted that the choice of 'cheapest deliverable' may change from time to time with obvious implications for futures market prices. As a rule of thumb, the cheapest deliverable is likely to be that stock out of the set of deliverable issues which has the highest gross redemption yield at any given point in time but this need not always be the case, particularly when some stocks are trading on an ex-dividend basis.

Currency futures

Essentially, currency futures are analogous to forward contracts in the foreign exchange market and their prices at any given time are linked to current spot rates by interest rate parity considerations. This is to say that if the markets are in equilibrium, the margin between spot and forward rates is a direct reflection of the differential between short-term interest rates in the two countries concerned.

Underlying this principle is the idea that, given a free and liquid market, a fixed-term investment in one currency must yield the same as a similar investment in a second currency, the recovery of which is secured at the outset by a currency swap transaction. These two alternative transactions are illustrated in Fig. 5.3.

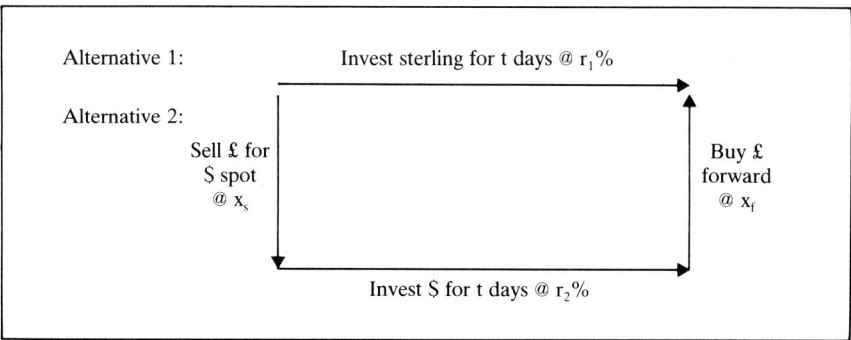

Fig. 5.3. Interest rate parity.

The proceeds of Alternative 1:

$$P\left(1 + \frac{r_1 t}{36,500}\right)$$

The proceeds of Alternative 2:

$$P \times X_s \left(1 + \frac{r_2 t}{36,000}\right) \times \frac{1}{X_f}$$

Arbitrage

If the two are identical:

$$\left(1 + \frac{r_1 t}{36{,}500}\right) = \frac{x_s}{x_f}\left(1 + \frac{r_2 t}{36{,}000}\right)$$

and $x_f = \dfrac{x_s \left(1 + \dfrac{r_2 t}{36{,}000}\right)}{\left(1 + \dfrac{r_1 t}{36{,}500}\right)}$

Having regard for the liquidity normally available in the foreign exchange market, we would expect this relationship to hold fairly tightly in practice and Table 5.6 shows this to be the case on 19 December 1985.

Table 5.6. Comparison of theoretical forward exchange rates and currency futures prices.

Futures delivery	Days from spot	Sterling rates (offer)	Eurodollar rates (offer)	Implied forward rates	LIFFE futures prices
Mar 1986	86	11.8125	8.0625	1.4107–15	1.4120
Jun 1986	177	11.875	8.0625	1.3980–97	1.4000
Sep 1986	268	11.75	8.0625	1.3874–98	1.3875

Spot rate: 1.4230.

As with our analysis of forward interest rates, we conclude that the futures market is trading very much in line with the cash market whilst, at the same time, for any given bid-offer spread in cash rates, the theoretical spread in the forward market broadens with increasing time to maturity.

This simple relationship can be expressed in a number of different ways to focus attention on each of its components and in these different forms it provides the basis of a wide variety of hedging, trading and arbitrage activities. Experience shows that it is relatively insensitive to modest day-to-day movements in interest rates although significant changes in one set of interest rates relative to the other, such as have been experienced when sterling has come under intense speculative pressure, for example, can have a dramatic impact on forward margins and hence on the spreads between successive futures contracts.

Some practical considerations

Before discussing in detail some of the more common arbitrage strategies pursued in the markets, it is appropriate to make some general – but none the less important – observations about the nature of arbitrage with financial futures and some of the practical considerations which must be borne in mind when attempting to translate theoretical price anomalies into profit.

In practice, it is almost impossible to close perfectly an arbitrage involving a financial futures contract. Because of their highly standardised specifications, it is not normally possible to match precisely the amounts and maturity dates of the transactions involved and, of course, this problem increases with the complexity of the strategy envisaged. Even on those occasions when exact cover is obtainable, it is not possible to forecast in advance the manner in which variation margin will accrue, and the eventual funding cost, or additional return associated with this daily flow of cash, will have a bearing on the final result. Let us consider these two important issues in turn.

Almost all arbitrages with futures are underpinned by the certainty that the price of each futures contract will, by definition, coincide with the price of the underlying cash market instrument or currency when the futures contract matures; this fundamental concept is at the heart of many hedging and trading strategies, too. In practice, however, it is not easy to obtain fine rates in the cash market for 'broken date' transactions designed to fit the futures delivery cycle so that a dealer must exercise his judgement to balance the theoretical improvement in margins he can obtain by dealing for conventional periods against the basis risk with which he will be faced if he does so. In certain circumstances, the design of the futures position can be refined to minimise basis risk (perhaps by dealing in strips of contracts, or straddles) but these techniques are not infallible and arbitrages undertaken on this basis should be monitored carefully and adjusted or closed out early if this becomes desirable.

In the main, arbitrage traders are not interested in the physical delivery process and will seek to close positions by undertaking offsetting transactions as soon as the realignment of the markets allows them to realise their profit in this manner. In most cash/futures arbitrages, however, the closure of the futures position must be accompanied by compensating transactions in the cash market which are required to preserve the arbitrage profit until the maturity of the original transactions. Unfortunately, this additional use of balance sheet resources has the effect of diluting the original profit perceived and thought must be given at the outset to the level of return which will be required to justify this extra commitment of resources.

Turning to the question of variation margin, all that can be said with certainty is that the effect of funding costs, or reinvestment income, will amplify the impact of futures price movements, for better or worse. However, if we assume that the price of a futures contract moves from its initial level, say P_0, to its closing level, P_1, in a totally random fashion, we can obtain a reasonable approximation of the funding cost, or reinvestment return associated with variation margin flows by asuming that this movement is totally linear. If r represents the average financing or reinvestment rate which should be applied (ideally we would like to distinguish between these rates but this is not feasible) then the expected interest on variation margin is proportional to the shaded areas in Figs. 5.4 and 5.5.

For currency futures contracts, the total variation margin and accrued interest at point B is approximately

$$(P_1 - P_0) \times \left(1 + \left(\frac{\frac{1}{2} r t_1}{360}\right)\right)$$

Arbitrage

and in order to compensate for this effect it is necessary to reduce the size of the futures position by a factor

$$\frac{1}{\left(1 + \frac{\frac{1}{2}rt_1}{360}\right)}$$

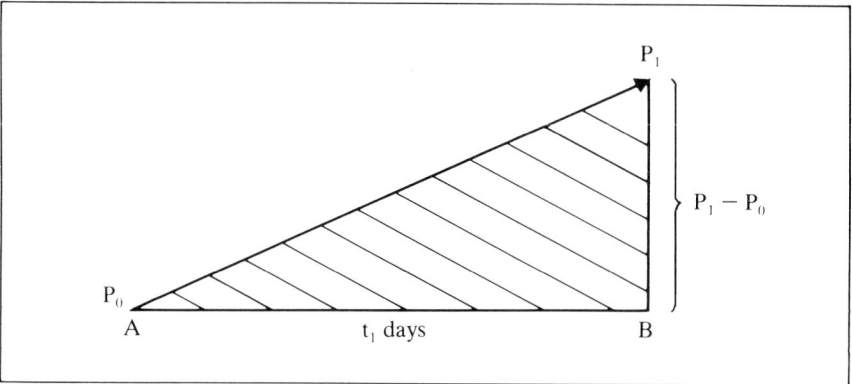

Fig. 5.4. The impact of interest on variation margin: currency futures.

For short-term deposit futures contracts, the effect is further magnified by the term of the deposit itself.

In this case, as illustrated in Fig. 5.5, the total variation margin and accrued interest at point C is

$$(P_1 - P_0) \times \left[1 + \frac{r(\frac{1}{2}t_1 + t_2)}{360*}\right]$$

*or 365 for a sterling-based contract

and for these contracts the variation margin leverage factor, as it is commonly called, is

$$\frac{1}{\left[1 + \frac{r(\frac{1}{2}t_1 + t_2)}{360}\right]}$$

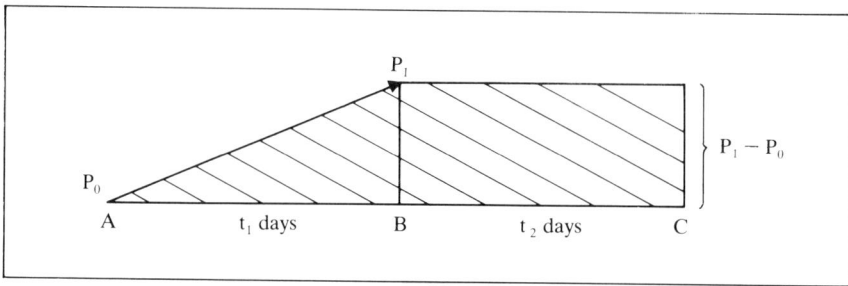

Fig. 5.5. The impact of interest on variation margin: short-term deposit futures.

Finally, we cannot ignore certain other transaction costs which can be foreseen from the outset, notably brokerage charges and the interest involved in financing initial margin requirements. Owing to competitive pressures, brokerage charges on the worlds' major futures exchanges are generally modest, particularly for high-volume generators of business such as professional arbitrageurs and traders. However, a commission rate of, say, $15 per contract per round trip, which is realistic in current market conditions, can represent a significant expense if a large number of futures contracts have to be dealt in the course of exploiting a marginal arbitrage opportunity. Similarly, although it is possible to lodge income-earning securities to cover initial margin requirements on most US exchanges, this is not yet generally feasible on LIFFE and at an interest rate of, say, 8%, the monthly cost of funding initial margin on currency contracts is

$$\$1{,}000 \times 0.08 \times \tfrac{1}{12} = \$6.67 \text{ (or 2.67 ticks) per contract.}$$

Due allowance for all these factors must be made at the outset when the viability of any proposed arbitrage is considered.

Simple intermarket arbitrage

Before embarking on a discussion of some of the more complex arbitrage strategies that can be pursued by dealers who have free access to a variety of instruments in different markets, it is appropriate for us to consider briefly some of the simplest forms of arbitrage that are commonly traded. These are straightforward intermarket transactions which may involve futures contracts only, or simultaneous transactions in both the futures and forward markets.

From the data contained in Appendix 1 (pages 84–85), it will be evident that a bank trader who wishes to establish a forward position in sterling for delivery on 19 March 1986 has a choice of at least three markets in which he can operate.

Table 5.7. Forward sterling rates on 19 December 1985 for delivery 19 March 1986.

Market	Price
Inter-bank	1.4100–10
LIFFE future	1.4115–20
IMM future	1.4110–15

Based on Table 5.7, a modest, but almost risk-free arbitrage profit can be achieved as follows:

> Buy £250,000 inter-bank forward at 1.4110 for a cost of $352,750.
> Sell 10 Mar 86 LIFFE sterling currency contracts at 1.4115 securing proceeds of $352,875.

Before expenses, this combination of transactions offers a profit of $125 when the positions mature in March 1986 at which time the sterling proceeds of the forward deal can be used to make delivery into the short futures

Arbitrage

position. Over time, the effects of further arbitrage of this nature will be to force the markets back into line with each other and in these circumstances the bank dealer will be looking to close his position by undertaking compensating transactions as soon as he can. Let us assume that he is able to do this in mid January 1986 when the markets have moved somewhat.

> Sell £250,000 inter-bank forward for delivery in March at 1.4750 generating proceeds of $368,750.
> Buy 10 Mar 86 LIFFE sterling currency contracts at 1.4750 equivalent to a cost of $368,750.

The result is as follows:

> Gain in forward market $368,750 − $352,750 = $16,000
> Loss on futures position 10 × 635 × $2.50 $15,875
> Net gain $125

Thus, the profit potential in the arbitrage can be realised in a number of ways and, indeed, the dealer may be able to improve upon this result if he is able to close out his position at a time when the futures market has become temporarily cheap compared with forward rates. In connection with this type of arbitrage, however, there are certain other points which are worthy of note:

1. Because both elements of the arbitrage are forward transactions, they have minimal impact upon the balance sheet and can be traded, therefore, fairly actively.
2. With an initial margin requirement of $1,000 per futures contract, the cost of supporting this position for any length of time can be material. At an interest rate of, say, 8% per annum, the monthly funding cost of $66.67 would soon erode the profit potential in the trade. It can be seen that these costs provide further incentive for the position to be closed out as quickly as possible.
3. The loss suffered in the futures market will have resulted in an outflow of variation margin which also has to be financed until the position is closed out. Once again, this additional cost can significantly erode the profit potential perceived at the outset if the size of the futures position is not effectively ratioed as discussed on pages 71–72.
4. For a non-member of the futures exchange, brokerage charges are likely to be in the order of $150.

It can readily be seen, therefore, that it is not necessarily worth while exploiting opportunities of this nature for very fine margins and those institutions who are members of futures exchanges and, therefore, able to clear their own transactions, are placed at a natural advantage in this type of business. In reality, dealers are likely to compromise the risk-free nature of this trade by dealing regularly in the markets, continually buying undervalued, and selling overvalued instruments, without necessarily attempting to execute both transactions simultaneously. Needless to say, they must be able to establish large positions in order to make this exercise worth while.

Financial futures

This type of arbitrage applies equally well to the interest rate futures contracts trading in Chicago and London where both the three-month Eurodollar and US Treasury Bond contracts trade simultaneously on two exchanges. A number of financial institutions which are members of both exchanges employ staff simply to trade in this manner. Telephone lines are kept open almost constantly throughout the trading day and although the profits available from this type of activity appear limited in relation to the resources committed, these very short-term trading activities improve the efficiency of the markets by providing a good deal of the liquidity which is needed to satisfy the requirements of other market participants.

More complex strategies

We now have the tools we need to consider more complex forms of arbitrage trading, involving both interest rate and currency futures contracts. In the previous section we compared the prices of currency futures contracts with equivalent rates available in the forward market. We will now develop this simple strategy by looking directly at the principal determinants of these forward rates and examining arbitrages between the spot and forward foreign exchange market and interest rates in the inter-bank market.

By way of illustration using the data in Appendix 1 (pages 84–85), let us consider the possibility that the price of the LIFFE Mar 86 sterling currency contract is too high. To exploit this opportunity, we would need to borrow US dollars until 19 March 1986, exchange them for sterling spot, lend this sterling in the market until 19 March 1986 and cover the repurchase of dollars with the sale of Mar 86 sterling currency futures contracts. This series of transactions is depicted diagramatically in Fig. 5.6. (Strictly speaking, we will also have to borrow sterling for a few days pending settlement of the Eurodollar transaction but for the purposes of this illustration we will ignore the additional cost involved which should be very small.)

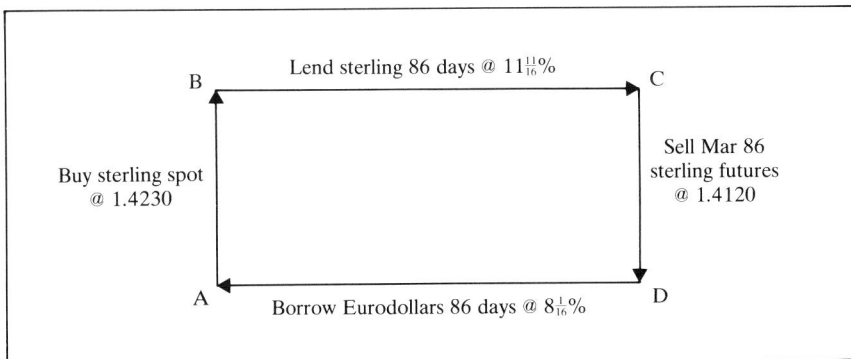

Fig. 5.6. Arbitrage between the foreign exchange, inter-bank and currency futures markets.

Given that these transactions are perfectly matched over time, we can evaluate the arbitrage potential by imagining that we borrow $1 at point A and proceed as follows:

Arbitrage

Transaction AB convert $1 at 1.4230 to £0.702741
BC lend £0.702741 for 86 days at $11\tfrac{1}{16}\%$:
proceeds £0.722093
CD convert £0.722093 at 1.4120 into $1.019595
DA repay borrowing of $1 at $8\tfrac{1}{16}\%$ for 86 days:
cost $1.019260

Arbitrage ratio $\dfrac{1.019595}{1.019260}$

$= 1.000328$

which is equivalent to $328 per $1 million borrowed, valued in December 1985. In simple cash terms, the surplus generated would be

$$\$1m \times (1.019595 - 1.019260) = \$335$$

per $1 million realised in March 1986.

A useful extension of this analysis involves the calculation of the sensitivity of the arbitrage ratio to movements in each of the transaction rates involved. This is achieved by calculating the change in each rate which would reduce the arbitrage ratio to unity, thus:

Sensitivity AB $(1.000328 - 1.000) \times 1.4230 = 0.00047$ or 4.7 ticks
BC $(1.000328 - 1.000) \times 365/86 = 0.00139$ or 13.9 bps
CD $(1.000328 - 1.000) \times 1.4120 = 0.00046$ or 4.6 ticks
DA $(1.000328 - 1.000) \times 360/86 = 0.00137$ or 13.9 bps

In other words, the sterling investment rate obtained, or dollar borrowing rate available could fall or rise respectively by almost 14 basis points before this slim arbitrage profit would be eliminated whilst a movement of less than 5 ticks in either of the currency rates would have the same effect. An important conclusion from these calculations is that, while the profit potential in this type of arbitrage is relatively insensitive to movements in interest rates, it is extremely sensitive to small changes in currency rates. It follows that transactions of this nature are really only relevant to those who have access to the finest of rates in the foreign exchange market.

As there is only one type of futures contract involved, it is not too difficult to establish a balanced position. Let us assume that a dealer borrows $5 million as the first leg of this arbitrage. The ideal sterling lending would be

$$5,000,000/1.4230 = £3,513,703$$

and the ideal number of futures contracts to be sold (allowing for the effect of interest on variation margin) would be

$$\frac{3513703 \left(1 + \dfrac{0.116875 \times 86}{365}\right)}{25,000} \times \frac{1}{\left(1 + \dfrac{0.080625 \times 43}{360}\right)}$$

$= 143$ contracts

Financial futures

The theoretical gain of $1,675 can be realised by holding the arbitrage until maturity of the futures contracts in March 1986. Over such an extended period, however, the cost of funding initial margin requirements would be significant and the dealer may well be tempted to lift his positions as soon as circumstances permit. However, as we have indicated previously, closing the cash positions before maturity will increase the balance sheet resources committed to this transaction and dilute its effective profitability. Thus it is necessary to assess the cost attributed to this additional use of resources so that the full implications of any decision to close out the position early can be taken into account.

In reality, the theoretical margin identified in this example would probably not be worth pursuing as an outright arbitrage, but a dealer may well decide to construct such a series of transactions if in the course of his ongoing commercial activities, one or other of the cash market transactions is presented to him.

Not only can futures contracts be arbitraged against spot foreign exchange rates and inter-bank deposit rates, but the same fundamental considerations can be projected off the balance sheet by examining the relationship between short-term deposit futures contracts and currency futures contracts for equivalent maturities. This type of arbitrage does not require access to the cash market and so can be traded fairly actively. The net variation margin flow represents the profit generated and so should be positive for most, if not all, of the holding period.

However, there are two main difficulties with futures/futures arbitrages of this type. Firstly, it is not easy to match the numbers of futures contracts required to obtain exact cover without creating very large positions to minimise the effects of rounding. Secondly, there is always the possibility that the markets will not have returned to equilibrium by the time that the nearby futures contracts mature. In these circumstances, the dealer must decide whether to accept a reduced profit (or even a loss) or convert his futures contracts into cash positions and run the arbitrage for a further period along the lines of our previous example.

Bearing in mind that currency futures straddles reflect three months interest rate differentials we can estimate that the prices of the LIFFE sterling currency contracts for Jun 86 and Sep 86 quoted on 19 December 1985 imply an interest rate differential of approximately 3.67% whilst the differential between the LIFFE short sterling and Eurodollar futures contracts for June delivery is only

$$92.14 - 88.76 = 3.38\%$$

This is an interesting anomaly and it may be exploited by selling Jun–Sep currency straddles and buying Jun Eurodollar–short sterling spreads as illustrated in Fig. 5.7. Assuming that these transactions can be perfectly matched and bearing in mind that the lending rate implied by the purchase of deposit futures contracts is 0.125% lower than the offer rate implied by the price quoted, the arbitrage ratio can be computed in four steps, as before:

Arbitrage

Transaction AB convert £1 at 1.4000 to $1.4000
BC lend $1.4000 91 days at 7.735%:
  proceeds $1.427373
CD convert $1.427373 at 1.3875 to £1.028738
DA repay borrowing of £1 at 11.24% for 91 days:
  cost £1.028023

Arbitrage ratio $\dfrac{1.028738}{1.028023} = 1.000696$

which is equivalent to £696 per £1 million borrowed at today's value. Alternatively, in simple cash terms, the profit potential is

£1m × (1.028738 − 1.028023) = £715 per £1m

realised in June.

In this instance, the sensitivities of this arbitrage gain to movements in the deposit and currency futures prices are approximately 28 basis points and 10 ticks respectively.

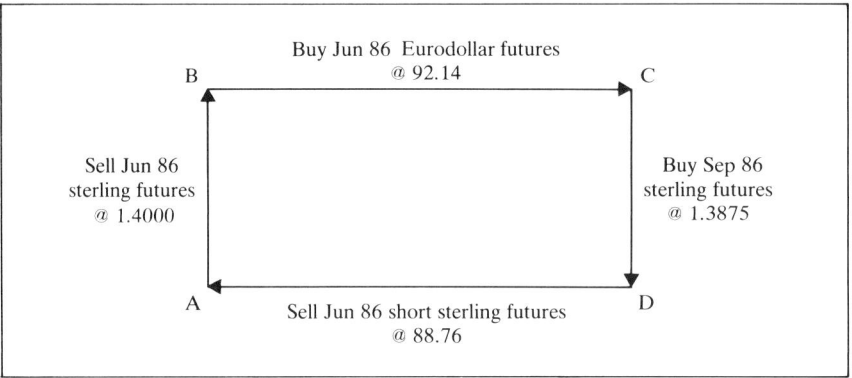

Fig. 5.7. Arbitrage between time deposit futures contracts and currency futures straddles.

Unfortunately, it is not an easy matter to construct an exactly balanced futures position to extract this perceived profit. If we assume that a dealer wishes to sell sufficient short sterling contracts to represent a borrowing of £10 million, the ideal numbers of futures contracts would be as follows:

Jun 86 short sterling:

$$\frac{10,000,000}{500,000} \times 91/90 \times \frac{1}{1 + 0.1124 \times \left(\dfrac{88.5 + 91}{365}\right)}$$

= 19.16 (or 19 contracts)

Sep 86 sterling currency:

$$\frac{10{,}000{,}000}{25{,}000} \times 91/90 \times \frac{1 + 0.0786 \times \left(\frac{88.5}{360}\right)}{1 + 0.0786 \times \left(\frac{88.5 + 91}{360}\right)}$$

$= 396.71$ (or 397 contracts)

Jun 86 Eurodollars:

$$\frac{10{,}000{,}000 \times 1.4}{1{,}000{,}000} \times 91/90 \times \frac{1}{1 + 0.0786 \times \left(\frac{88.5 + 91}{360}\right)}$$

$= 13.62$ (or 14 contracts)

Jun 86 sterling currency:

$$396.71 \times \frac{1.3875}{1.4000} = 393.17 \text{ (or 393 contracts)}$$

An arbitrage constructed with these ratios should have minimal exposure to changes in futures prices. Let us assume, for example, that the markets are exactly in equilibrium on 16 June 1986 at the following prices:

Spot sterling: $1.35
Eurodollar futures: 92.00
Short sterling futures: 89.00
implying a three-month forward exchange rate of $1.3405

The result of closing out the futures contracts would be as follows:

Sold 19 Jun short sterling at 88.76, bought back at 89.00
19 × (8,876 − 8,900) × £12.50 = −£5,700

Bought 397 Sep currency futures at 1.3875, sold at 1.3405
397 × (1.3405 − 1.2875) × 25,000 = $466,475

Bought 14 Jun Eurodollars at 92.14, sold at 92.00
14 × (9,200 − 9,214) × $25 = −$4,900

Sold 393 Jun currency futures at 1.4000, bought back at 1.3500
393 × (1.4000 − 1.3500) × 25,000 = +$491,250

Converting the net dollar profit at spot rates at that time would give a net profit of £9,022, very much in line with the dealer's original expectations. In an exactly similar fashion, it can be demonstrated that the arbitrage profit should be preserved even in the event of a significant appreciation in the sterling/US dollar exchange rate.

Once again, however, allowance has yet to be made for transaction costs which are likely to be considerable, having regard for the significant number of futures contracts dealt and the extended period for which initial margin must be funded. Some relief is possible in the form of reduced margin

Arbitrage

requirements for the currency straddles ($100 per pair of contracts) but, even so, this type of arbitrage is likely to appeal mainly to members of futures exchanges who can minimise the execution and clearing costs involved.

Given the wide range of futures instruments and delivery dates available, it can be seen that the basic principles involved in these two examples can be extended in any number of ways. In particular, subject to certain assumptions, the deposit futures employed to secure forward short-term interest rates can be replaced by long gilt or US Treasury Bond straddles, the values of which also imply short-term interest rates. Having said this, the greater the variety of contracts employed, the greater will be the problem of mismatches and transaction costs, and there comes a point beyond which the search for further complexity is unlikely to bear fruit in practical terms.

Synthetic instruments and proxy currencies

The calculations we have completed thus far lead us to the general conclusion that, complex though some relationships may be, prices of the cash and futures instruments we have examined are essentially in line with each other. Unless a trading institution has some inherent advantage in the markets in which it operates (perhaps because of the quality of its name or its market-making capability), worthwhile arbitrage profits are not easily made unless some degree of trading risk is accepted. In practical terms, therefore, interest rate and currency futures are likely to find more widespread application in risk management situations where, although the motivation behind each transaction may be different, the arbitrage techniques we have discussed are directly relevant.

In this section we turn our attention to the management of interest rates in the currencies for which there are no interest rate futures available. We consider a synthetic borrowing or lending to be a combination of cash and futures instruments which is designed to produce the best possible interest rate for a given period or to offer greater liquidity or flexibility than a straightforward cash market transaction. If it is necessary to switch into a second currency to achieve this objective, the new currency involved is called a proxy currency. The opportunities for using synthetics and proxies may be more frequent than outright arbitrages because these techniques are used to meet existing business requirements as opposed to pure arbitrage which is normally carried out in addition to these activities.

In terms of rate enhancement, the successful use of synthetic instruments and proxy currencies depends upon the identification of modest discrepancies between futures prices and their theoretical values. For the reasons we have discussed, these are most likely to be found among the short-term deposit interest rate contracts.

Let us consider, for example, the case of a West German manufacturing company which is borrowing DM10 million in the Eurocurrency market and is seeking to protect the rate it must pay on the next three months' rollover of this borrowing which is due on 3 March 1986. Theoretically, the treasurer could obtain this protection by creating a forward/forward borrowing as described on page 45. As an alternative, however, he could sell some Mar 86 Eurodollar futures and cover the exchange risk by buying Mar–Jun 86 currency futures straddles. The mechanics of this alternative series of transactions are depicted in Fig. 5.8.

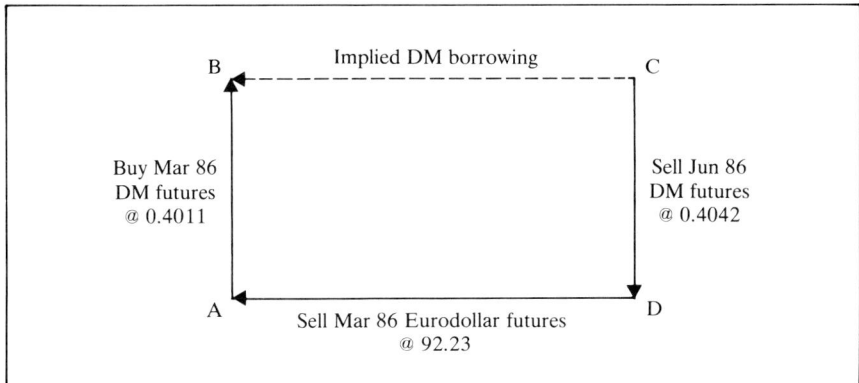

Fig. 5.8. Construction of a synthetic Deutschmark forward borrowing.

As before, we can assess the theoretical Deutschmark borrowing rate implied by these futures transactions by considering the gain involved in each leg, as follows:

$$\text{Transaction CD} = 0.4042$$

$$\text{DA} \quad \frac{1}{\left(1 + 0.0777 \times \frac{92}{360}\right)} = 0.980530$$

$$\text{AB} \quad \frac{1}{0.4011} = 2.493144$$

creating an overall gain of

$$\text{CD} \times \text{DA} \times \text{AB} = 0.988108$$

which implies an effective Deutschmark borrowing rate r, such that

$$\left(\frac{1}{1 + \frac{r.92}{360}}\right) = 0.988108$$
$$r = 4.71\%$$

The ratioing techniques required to implement this futures position are virtually identical to those discussed on pages 76–77 and need not be repeated here.

By comparison, the forward/forward Deutschmark borrowing rate implied by borrowing in the cash market for 162 days at $4\frac{7}{8}\%$ and simultaneously lending for 70 days at $4\frac{1}{4}\%$ is 4.92%, or some 21 basis points higher than the synthetic alternative. Having said this, of course, the treasurer has still to take into account transaction costs and the basis risk associated with the fact that his futures positions will have to be lifted sometime before

Arbitrage

maturity. These risks should not be large, however, and can be set against the fact that the forward/forward alternative would use up credit lines and tie up balance sheet resources in an unwelcome fashion. If there is insufficient liquidity available in the futures market, a forward foreign exchange swap could be used alongside the Eurodollar futures position to achieve very similar results.

Under different circumstances, the same company may have surplus funds available for investment in the Eurodollar–Deutschmark market and, once again, a synthetic form of investment may enable the treasurer to improve upon the yield available from a straightforward cash market transaction. Let us assume that, instead of worrying about borrowing rates on 19 December 1985, the treasurer has surplus Deutschmarks available for investment for a period of roughly six months.

In the inter-bank market, he could obtain a risk-free rate of $4\frac{3}{4}\%$ which would also be free of transaction costs. However, one synthetic alternative he may wish to consider is an initial investment for only 86 days with the reinvestment rate for the next 91 days secured by the purchase of Mar 86 Eurodollar futures and the sale of Mar–Jun 86 currency futures straddles. These two alternative strategies are illustrated in Fig. 5.9.

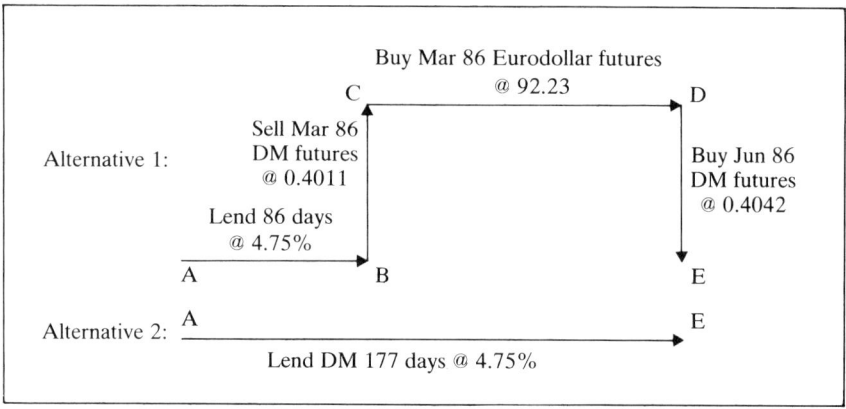

Fig. 5.9. Construction of a synthetic six months' Deutschmark investment.

Once again, we can calculate the Deutschmark investment rate implied by this series of transactions by examining the gain involved in each leg.

$$\text{Transaction AB } 1 + 0.0475 \times \frac{86}{360} = 1.011347$$

$$\text{BC} = 0.4011$$

$$\text{CD } 1 + 0.07645 \times \frac{91}{360} = 1.019325$$

$$\text{DE } \frac{1}{0.4042} = 2.474023$$

Creating an overall gain of

$$\text{AB} \times \text{BC} \times \text{CD} \times \text{DE} = 1.022985$$

which implies a Deutschmark investment rate r, such that

$$1 + r \times \frac{177}{360} = 1.022985$$
$$r = 4.67\%$$

In this instance, clearly the treasurer would prefer to adopt Alternative 2. This result is not surprising, of course, having regard to our earlier findings which suggested that the price of the Mar 86 Eurodollar future is high enough to offer some arbitrage potential from the sellers point of view. In such circumstances it is most unlikely to represent particularly good value from the standpoint of an investor. Interestingly, our usual sensitivity analysis suggests that the price of the Eurodollar contract would have to fall by 15 basis points to 92.08 in order to make this strategy worth while, all other rates being unchanged.

As we have intimated previously, there are almost always modest residual risks associated with the creation of synthetic instruments of this nature and the design of the balanced futures positions required to preserve the theoretical margins identified is not a simple matter. Nevertheless, situations frequently arise in which the rate improvement obtainable, coupled with the increased flexibility offered by this type of strategy, outweighs the risks involved. On the basis of the principles employed in these examples it is not difficult to establish computerised support systems which can be used to survey the wide range of strategies available on a regular basis.

Conclusion

Reflecting for a moment on the foregoing sections of this chapter, we are forced to the conclusion that although the basic concepts of arbitrage with financial futures may be simple, the trading strategies involved in applying these concepts are far from straightforward and rarely perfect. Additionally, now that the futures markets are reaching maturity in many ways, genuine price anomalies are usually small and short-lived. In order to generate worthwhile profits from this type of activity, an arbitrage trader must be prepared to establish large positions and control them carefully.

This does not imply, however, that financial futures contracts have little value to professional dealers seeking to enhance returns from their traditional operations in the foreign exchange and money markets on a low risk basis. In fact, the introduction of these new instruments has added a new dimension to the range of trading opportunities available and the flexibility associated with dealing in the futures markets can have considerable practical advantages in many situations.

From a wider perspective, too, it is clear that the arbitrage relationships we have discussed have a major bearing on price determination in the futures markets so that careful consideration of these relationships is essential for those who are preparing to make use of futures contracts for hedging or more speculative trading purposes. In the long run, time spent on this study will not go unrewarded.

Arbitrage

Appendices

APPENDIX 1 – DATA FOR EXAMPLES

The following data represent a snapshot of the state of the cash and futures markets at approximately 2.30 p.m. on Thursday, 19 December 1985. There is nothing significant in the choice of this time, save for the fact that the US and European markets were operating alongside each other and prices were fairly stable. Market conditions, therefore, were not exceptional in any way and it is reasonable to suppose that the prices and rates recorded should have been in equilibrium with each other. As far as it is possible to judge, therefore, any arbitrage opportunities identified from this data should have been realisable in practice.

(i) London inter-bank deposit market – offered rates (%)

Term	Eurodollars	Sterling	Euro DM	Euro SF
One month	$8\frac{1}{8}$	$11\frac{3}{4}$	$4\frac{13}{16}$	$4\frac{1}{2}$
Two months	$8\frac{1}{16}$	$11\frac{13}{16}$	$4\frac{7}{8}$	$4\frac{5}{16}$
Three months	$8\frac{1}{16}$	$11\frac{13}{16}$	$4\frac{7}{8}$	$4\frac{1}{4}$
Six months	$8\frac{1}{16}$	$11\frac{7}{8}$	$4\frac{7}{8}$	$4\frac{3}{16}$
Nine months	$8\frac{1}{16}$	$11\frac{3}{4}$	$4\frac{7}{8}$	$4\frac{3}{16}$
Twelve months	$8\frac{1}{8}$	$11\frac{3}{4}$	$4\frac{15}{16}$	$4\frac{3}{16}$

(ii) Foreign exchange market – mid rates

Period	£/US$	DM/US$	DM/£
Spot	1.4230	2.5130	3.5770
One month	1.4188	2.5058	3.5562
Two months	1.4140	2.4990	3.5348
Three months	1.4100	2.4930	3.5164
Six months	1.3978	2.4730	3.4579
Nine months	1.3879	2.4550	3.4087
Twelve months	1.3780	2.4370	3.3595

(iii) Fixed interest securities – offered prices

(a) UK gilt market (32nds)
Treasury $11\frac{1}{2}\%$ 19 Mar 2001/4 – 109–11
Treasury $13\frac{1}{2}\%$ 26 Mar 2004/8 – 126–08

(b) US Treasury Bond market (32nds)
  $9\frac{7}{8}\%$ Bond 2015   – 104–12
  $10\frac{5}{8}\%$ Bond 2015   – 110–00
  $11\frac{3}{4}\%$ Bond 2014   – 118–20

(iv) Short-term interest rate futures

Contract month	LIFFE Eurodollar	IMM Eurodollar	LIFFE short sterling
Mar 86	92.23	92.23	88.36
Jun 86	92.14	92.15	88.76
Sep 86	91.92	91.92	88.95
Dec 86	91.64	91.62	88.94

(v) Currency futures

Contract month	LIFFE BP	IMM BP	LIFFE DM	IMM DM
Mar 86	1.4120	1.4115	0.4011	0.4011
Jun 86	1.4000	1.3995	0.4042	0.4041
Sep 86	1.3875	1.3870	0.4076	0.4074

(vi) Futures on long-term fixed coupon securities

(a) LIFFE long gilt contract (32nds)

Contract month	
Mar 86	110–23
Jun 86	111–03

(b) CBT Treasury Bond contract (32nds)

Contract month	
Mar 86	83–24
Jun 86	82–22
Sep 86	81–26
Dec 86	81–04

APPENDIX 2 – SUMMARY OF CONTRACT SPECIFICATIONS

(i) Interest rate futures

Contract (exchange)	3-month Eurodollar (IMM, LIFFE and SIMEX)	Short sterling (LIFFE)	US Treasury bond (CBT and LIFFE)	Twenty-year gilt (LIFFE)
Unit of trading	$1 million	£500,000	$100,000 notional bond with 8% coupon	£50,000 notional gilt with 12% coupon
Contract standard	Cash settlement based on 3-month LIBOR on last trading day	Cash settlement based on 3-month LIBOR on last trading day	Delivery of eligible Treasury bond with minimum 15 years to maturity or first call date	Delivery of eligible gilt with 15–25 years to maturity
Delivery dates	Third Wednesday of delivery month	Third Wednesday of delivery month	Any business day in delivery month	Any business day in delivery month
Delivery months	Mar, Jun, Sep, Dec	Mar, Jun, Sep, Dec	Mar, Jun, Sep, Dec	Mar, Jun, Sep, Dec
Last trading day	11.00 two business days before 3rd Wednesday of delivery month	11.00 third Wednesday of delivery month	15.00 seven business days prior to last business day of delivery month	11.00 two business days prior to last business day of delivery month
Price quotation	100 – interest rate	100 – interest rate	Per $100 par value	Per £100 nominal
Minimum price movement (value)	0.01 ($25)	0.01 (£12.50)	$\frac{1}{32}$ ($31.25)	£$\frac{1}{32}$ (£15.625)
Initial margin	$1,000	£500	$2,000 (CBT) $1,250 (LIFFE)	£1,000
Trading hours (London times)	13.20–20.00 (IMM) 08.30–16.00 (LIFFE) 02.00–09.20 (SIMEX)	08.20–16.02	14.00–20.00 (CBT) 08.15–16.10 (LIFFE)	09.30–16.15

(ii) Currency futures

Contract (exchange)	British pound (IMM and LIFFE)	Deutschmark (IMM and LIFFE)	Swiss franc (IMM and LIFFE)	Japanese yen (IMM and LIFFE)
Unit of trading	£25,000	DM125,000	SF125,000	¥12,500,000
Contract standard	Currencies concerned are deliverable in principal financial centres of countries of issue based upon official settlement prices on last trading day.			
Delivery dates	Third Wednesday of delivery month			
Delivery months	March, June, September, December*			
Last trading day	Two business days prior to delivery day			
Price quotation	US$ per £	US$ per DM	US$ per SF	US$ per ¥100
Minimum price movement (value)	0.05c per £ ($12.50) IMM 0.01c per £ ($2.50) LIFFE	0.01c per DM ($12.50)	0.01c per SF ($12.50)	0.01c per ¥100 ($12.50)
Initial margin	$1,000	$1,000	$1,000	$1,000
Trading hours (London times)	13.30–19.24 (IMM) 08.32–16.02 (LIFFE)	13.30–19.20 (IMM) 08.34–16.04 (LIFFE)	13.30–19.16 (IMM) 08.36–16.06 (LIFFE)	13.30–19.28 (IMM) 08.30–16.00 (LIFFE)

* Certain intermediate delivery months are available on the IMM but, generally, these are not actively traded.

CHAPTER 6

Currency options

Jeryl Hack

In the early 1980s, currency options were introduced to the foreign exchange market. At first, the market in this instrument developed slowly. Then, in 1982, standardised currency options began trading at publicly quoted exchanges and interest in the product grew dramatically. Today there are at least six major exchanges trading currency options and an active over-the-counter options market has developed within the international foreign exchange dealing network.

Even though considerable attention has been focused on this market during the past three years, currency option trading is still in its infancy. Only a small proportion of foreign exchange market participants are fully conversant with the use of options as a tool in their currency exposure management, and it will take time before the full potential of the currency options market can be realised.

The aim of this chapter is to introduce currency options to those who wish to develop a working knowledge of the instrument. This presentation begins with a review of the development of the currency options market. Then fundamental aspects of currency option pricing will be discussed and the influence of arbitrage on the pricing and trading of options will be examined. Finally, the most frequently employed options trading and hedging strategies will be described.

Background

Since 1972 and the end of the fixed rate foreign exchange system, the management of foreign exchange exposures has become increasingly difficult. As the volatility of the foreign exchange markets has increased so have the currency risks associated with international trade and finance. By the late 1970s, the foreign exchange customers of major banks began asking for a foreign exchange product which would provide a new risk management capability and be better suited for handling their foreign exchange exposures: in essence, today's currency option.

Banks initially became involved in the currency option market because of their own client demand for the product. At first, only a few banks offered currency options to their customers, and this was on a limited basis. It was not long, however, before several major banks introduced currency options as part of their regular foreign exchange service. Given the competitive nature of the foreign exchange market, it is not surprising that many other banks entered the currency option market because of concerns that their foreign exchange client base would be threatened if they were unable to offer currency options to clients.

It was natural for foreign exchange traders with little knowledge of options to price currency options at levels which seemed reasonable, given their view of where the exchange rate would be during the life of the option. Pricing in this manner however, did not accurately reflect the value of an option or take into account the need to manage option positions. After a number of banks suffered significant losses, it became apparent that traders needed to combine their foreign exchange experience with a thorough understanding of options in order to price and manage currency option positions effectively.

Information about currency options during the initial phase of the market's development was scarce. A significant knowledge gap existed between the foreign exchange and option markets. Foreign exchange traders had never been exposed to options and option traders knew very little about foreign exchange. The problem was compounded by the fact that most of the academic studies of options related to options on stocks and there are signficant differences between stock and currency options.

With time and growing market interest, information about currency options became more readily available. By 1983, academic research relating to the pricing of currency options had been published and was being closely studied by option traders. Computer software was developed to price and manage currency options. These systems helped the banks involved in the market to price and manage currency option positions more effectively and also proved to be an important educational tool for institutions preparing to enter the market.

The introduction of currency option trading on publicly quoted exchanges in 1982 also had a significant impact on the market's development. The exchanges made it possible for foreign exchange and option traders to interact in the market-place and this helped to close the knowledge gap between the foreign exchange and option markets mentioned previously. Through the marketing efforts of the exchanges, many potential users of currency options were introduced to the product and this ultimately led to increased liquidity in the market-place. Exchange traded options also gave the banks a means of offsetting some of the risks associated with their currency option activity in the over-the-counter market. With these expanded educational and risk management resources, it did not take long for a number of banks to become experienced and professional currency option traders.

Today, average daily currency option trading volume is estimated at more than $5 billion. In addition to the activity of banks, the involvement and interest of corporate treasurers managing foreign exchange exposure, commercial concerns involved in international trade, international fund managers, trading firms and individual speculators have contributed to the growth of the market.

In the short term, many of these market participants are able to enter the market after simply understanding what a currency option is and deciding whether to buy or sell the option based on a price evaluation and/or currency outlook. In the longer term, however, a more comprehensive understanding of the instrument is needed.

An effective approach taken by those who wish to learn about currency options involves three major steps. The first is a study of basic option terminology and the market profiles of buyers and sellers of options. Secondly, attention must be given to fundamental aspects of currency options pricing and the influence of arbitrage on pricing and trading. Finally, an understanding of frequently employed option trading and hedging strategies should be developed.

Currency options defined

Currency options provide option buyers with the right, rather than the obligation, to buy or sell foreign exchange during a specified period of time or on a fixed date.

The buyer of a call option pays a premium and is granted the right to purchase a specified amount of currency at a fixed price. The call seller (writer) receives the premium and is then obliged to deliver currency at the call holder's request.

The buyer of a put option pays a premium and is granted the right to sell a currency at a fixed price. The put seller receives the premium and is obliged to purchase the currency at the put holder's request.

While spot, forward and future foreign exchange transactions all establish fixed rate currency deals, foreign exchange options permit the buyer of an option to 'walk away' from the currency transaction if it is not wanted or needed. The maximum risk faced by the option buyer is the initial cost of the option.

Option terminology

Most financial markets have a tendency to develop market 'jargon' which can make relatively simple concepts appear complex or difficult to understand. The options market can be accused of having this problem. Initially, it is important to be familiar with the terms which relate to the currency option itself, including the following:

Underlying currency. The currency which the option buyer has the right to purchase or to sell.

Base currency. The currency in which the cost of the option is paid and against which the underlying currency is traded.

Strike price/Exercise price. The price at which the foreign exchange deal will be transacted if the option is exercised.

Premium. The price of the option.

Expiration date. The date on which the option expires.

American option. The option which can be exercised at any time prior to the expiration date.

European option. The option which can only be exercised on the expiration date.

Option market profiles

To understand various market positions, option traders frequently graph the profit/loss (P/L) profiles on an option. A call buyer, for example, has the right to establish a long position in the underlying currency. If the exchange rate exceeds the exercise price at expiration, the option has value. If the exchange rate is less than the exercise price, the option will be worthless.

A graph of a call holder's P/L profile at expiration is illustrated in Fig. 6.1.*

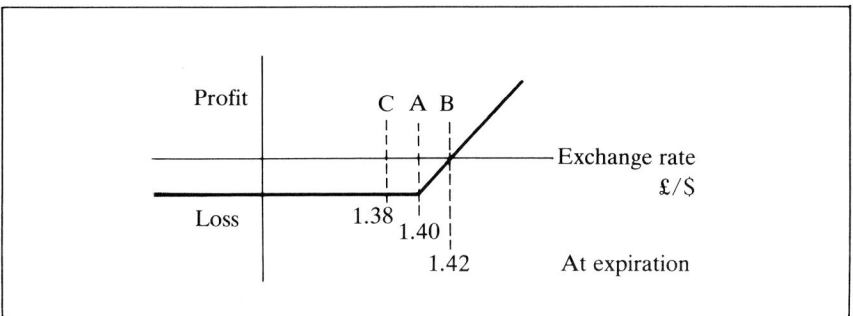

Fig. 6.1. Call P/L profile.

>Buy a sterling $1.40 call at 2 cents per pound.
>At an exchange rate of $1.40 (point A), the call has no value and the call buyer faces the loss of the entire premium paid for the option.
>At the exchange rate of $1.42 (point B), which equates to the strike price of the option plus the premium paid, the call buyer will break even on the option deal.
>Above the exchange rate of $1.42, the call position is profitable.

It is clear from Fig. 6.1 that the maximum risk faced by the call holder is the initial premium paid for the option. It is also important to notice that if a call has been established to hedge a foreign exchange exposure, at exchange rates below $1.38 (point C), the ability to purchase pounds sterling at a lower rate in the cash markets can be viewed as offsetting the initial cost of the option.

A put buyer holds the right to sell currency at the exercise price of the option. A graph of a put holder's P/L profile at expiration is shown in Fig. 6.2.

---

* Commissions and transaction costs are not included in the calculations in this chapter.

Arbitrage

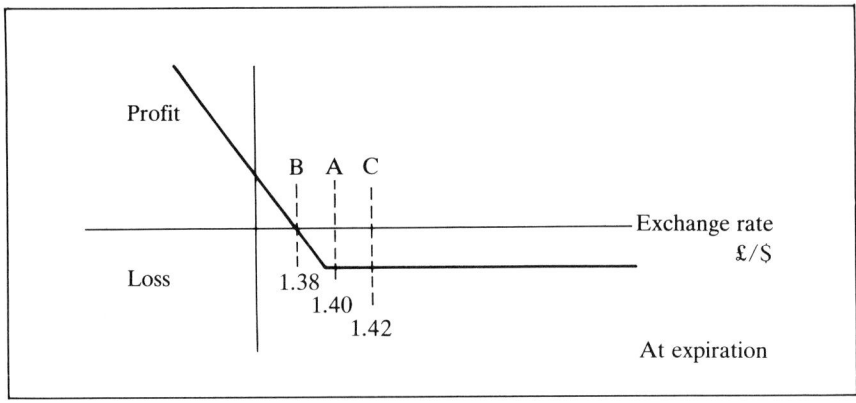

Fig. 6.2. Put P/L profile.

Buy a sterling $1.40 put at 2 cents per pound.

At the exchange rate of $1.40 (point A), the put will expire worthless and the put buyer will face the loss of the initial premium paid for the option.

At a rate of $1.38 (point B), which equates to the strike price minus the premium paid for the option, the put buyer will 'break-even'.

Below $1.38, the put position will be profitable.

As in the case of the call, if the put has been established as a hedge and the exchange rate is above $1.42, the ability to sell sterling at higher rate in the cash markets offsets the initial cost of the option. The maximum risk of the put position is the premium paid for the option.

As familiarity with the P/L profiles grows, it is possible to observe important relationships between the cash and option foreign exchange markets.

A long cash foreign exchange position will have a P/L profile similar to that shown in Fig. 6.3.

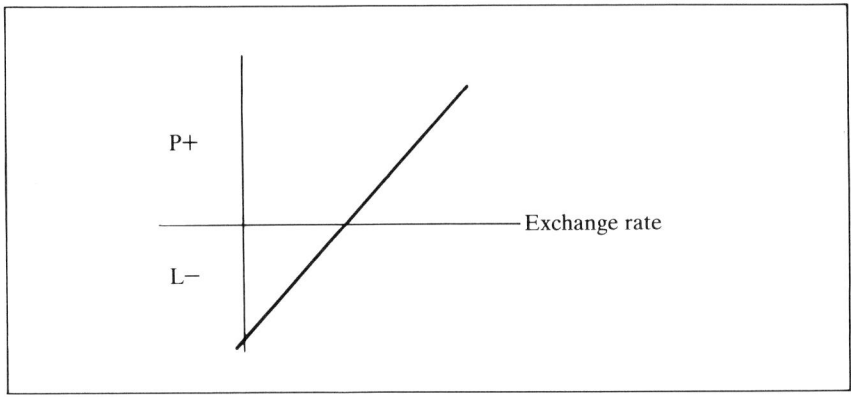

Fig. 6.3.

By combining the P/L profile of a long call option with that of a short put option, it is possible to derive the same P/L profile, as shown in Fig. 6.4.

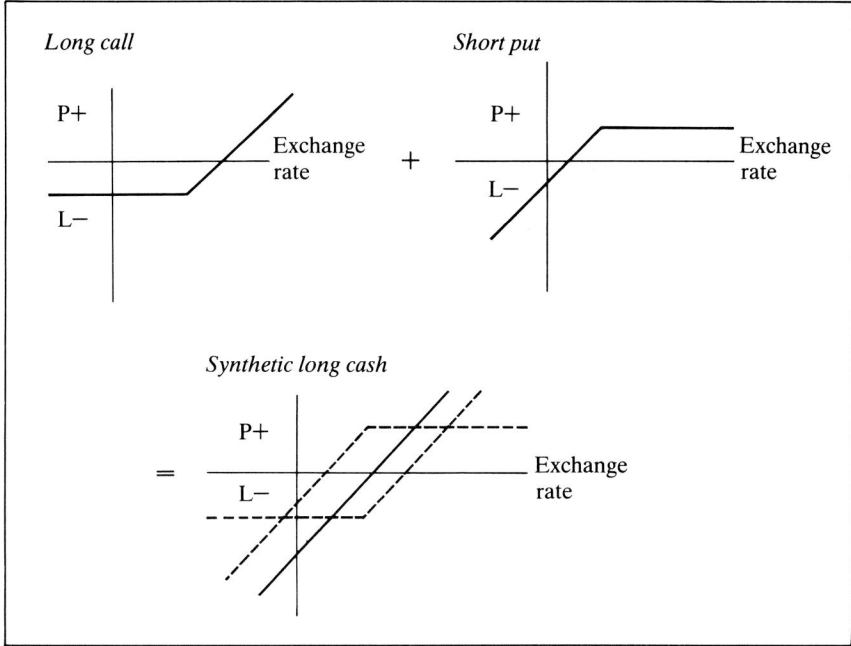

Fig. 6.4.

If sterling appreciates, the call and the long cash position will be profitable. If sterling declines in value, the short put and the long cash position will both result in losses. The combination of a long call and short put is effectively equivalent to a long cash currency position.

In a similar fashion, a short cash position P/L profile can be replicated by establishing a long put and short call position (Fig. 6.5).

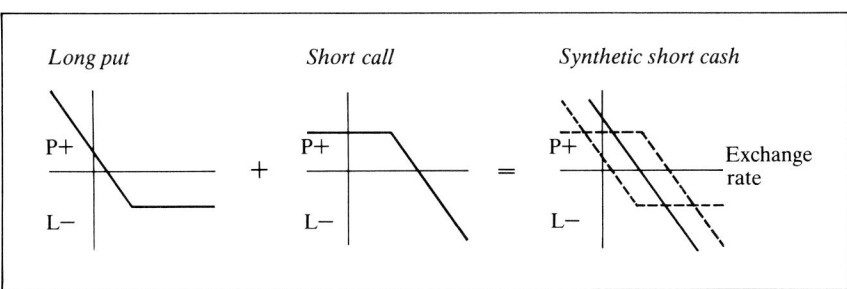

Fig. 6.5.

If sterling declines in value, the short cash position and the put are both profitable. If sterling appreciates, the short cash position and the short call will both result in losses.

Using P/L profiles it also becomes clear that a call can be replicated by establishing a long cash position and a long put position (Fig. 6.6).

Arbitrage

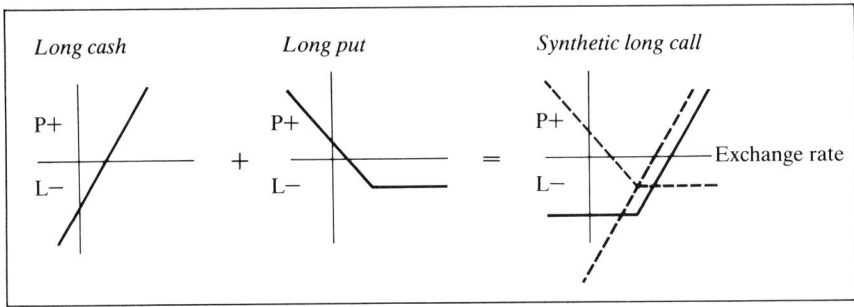

Fig. 6.6.

As the price of sterling rises, the call and the long cash position are profitable. As sterling declines in value, the call loss is limited to the initial premium paid and the profit on the put offsets the losses accruing on the long cash position.

Finally, it is possible to create a put position by selling cash foreign exchange and buying a call (Fig. 6.7).

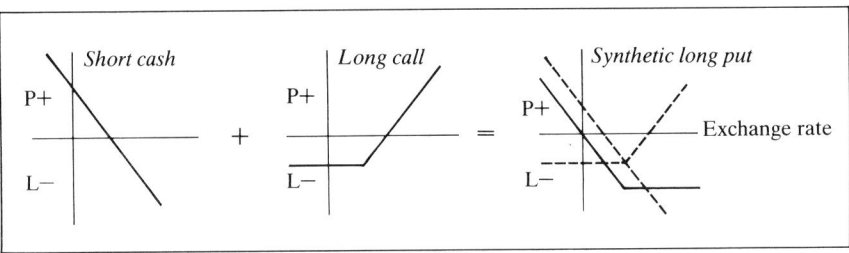

Fig. 6.7.

As sterling declines in value, the put as well as the short cash position are profitable. As sterling appreciates, the put loss is limited to the initial premium paid for the option and the long call profit offsets losses accruing on the short cash position.

The equivalence of combinations of option and cash positions has important implications for option pricing. Since option and cash positions can be established which replicate each other, the cost of the synthetic positions created by combining these instruments must be in line with the price of the original position. When this is not the case, a trader can buy in one market and sell in another and profit from a riskless arbitrage opportunity.

If, for example, a long cash position costs more than the cost of buying a call and selling a put, option traders will establish the option's synthetic long position and sell cash foreign exchange until market prices come into line with one another. Likewise, if a short cash position can be replicated by buying a put and selling a call at a rate higher than the exchange rate, market traders will sell the synthetic short position and buy in the cash market until the riskless profit is no longer available.

These market relationships form boundary pricing parameters between option prices and the underlying exchange rates, as well as between calls and puts. (The fact that American options can be exercised early introduces variations to these relationships which are not examined in this discussion.) Market prices are thus kept in line by professional traders who will take advantage of such arbitrage opportunities whenever prices are out of line.

Option pricing

To understand how an individual option is priced, it is necessary to separate the option's value into two major components;

1. Intrinsic value.
2. Time value.

Intrinsic value

Intrinsic value refers to the amount an option is worth if it is exercised and the underlying currency is bought or sold at the prevailing exchange rate. Assume the spot sterling rate is $1.45. The owner of a sterling $1.40 call can exercise the call to buy sterling at $1.40. It is then possible for him to sell sterling in the spot market at $1.45. The intrinsic value of the call is thus $0.05.

Sterling spot rate	$1.45
Sterling call strike	$1.40
Intrinsic value	$0.05

The intrinsic value of a call option is the amount by which the exchange rate exceeds the option's stike price.

If the sterling spot rate is $1.35, the owner of a sterling $1.40 put can exercise the put to sell sterling at $1.40 and at the same time purchase sterling in the cash market at $1.35 to gain $0.05. Therefore the intrinsic value of this option is also $0.05.

Sterling put strike	$1.40
Sterling spot rate	$1.35
Intrinsic value	$0.05

The intrinsic value of a put option is the amount by which the option strike price exceeds the exchange rate.

Suppose that both of these options were priced at $0.04. In the case of the call, the holder of the option would buy sterling for a total cost of $1.44 (strike price + premium) by exercising the call immediately and be able to sell sterling in the cash market at $1.45. This would lock-in a guaranteed profit to the option holder of $0.01. The holder of the put, with the spot rate at $1.35, could sell sterling at $1.36 (strike price − premium) by exercising the put and buy spot at $1.35, thereby gaining $0.01. From these examples it should be clear that if an option is priced at less than its intrinsic value a riskless arbitrage opportunity is created. In an efficient market, arbitrageurs will take advantage of this situation until the cost of the option reflects, at a minimum, its intrinsic value.

Currency options are frequently described relative to the amount of intrinsic value they hold. An option which has intrinsic value is called an 'in-the-money' option. An option which has a strike price that is equal to the exchange rate of the underlying currency, is referred to as an 'at-the-money' option. An option which does not have any intrinsic value is known as an 'out-of-the-money' option.

Example

Sterling spot rate at $1.40

Strike	Call		Put
$1.35	In	the money	Out of
$1.40	At		At
$1.45	Out of		In

Time value

Time value is the second component of a currency option's price. Although time value is often misconstrued as being exclusively a function of the time to expiration of the option, it also reflects the other variables which influence whether or not the currency option will become valuable prior to its expiration.

The most significant of these variables are strike price, volatility, interest rates, and market supply and demand.

TIME TO EXPIRATION

The longer the life of an option the greater the possibility that the option will become valuable before expiration. Therefore, the prices of options with long expiration dates will be greater than those with near-term expiration dates.

Example

Sterling $1.45 Call

2 months	$0.020
5 months	$0.034
8 months	$0.043
11 months	$0.050

STRIKE PRICE

An option has the greatest time value when it is at-the-money and time value decreases for options that are increasingly in- or out-of-the-money. This is because there is the greatest uncertainty as to whether or not an at-the-money option will be exercised, whereas a deep in-the-money option has a high probability of being exercised, and a far out-of-the-money option has a low possibility of being exercised.

MARKET SUPPLY AND DEMAND

Market supply and demand for an option may influence its price in the short term. Over time, however, arbitrage opportunities will arise which will eventually cause prices to reflect accurately the variables previously discussed.

AN OPTION AS A WASTING ASSET

During the life of an option, its price is a function of its intrinsic value and time value. At expiration, however, the option will only be worth its intrinsic value. Because time value declines to 0 at expiration, an option is a wasting asset.

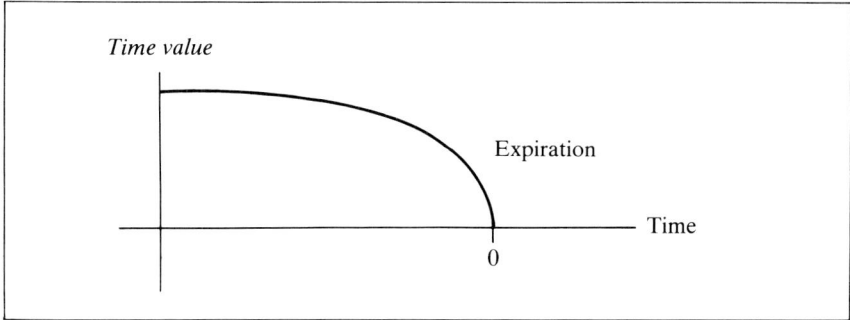

Fig. 6.8. Option time delay.

Time value does not decline in a linear fashion, but at an exponential rate. During the life of an option, the decrease in time value accelerates. This accounts for the curve of the graph of time value (Fig. 6.8).

VOLATILITY

Volatility reflects the magnitude of change in an underlying exchange rate. The greater the volatility of an exchange rate, the more the time value of the option. An option writer will demand to be paid more for an option on a volatile currency than on a stable currency.

The historical volatility of a currency is a statistical measure of the magnitude of changes in the daily spot exchange rates during a specified period of time. Implied volatility reflects what the market perceives the volatility of a currency to be. It is calculated by taking the market price of a specific option, together with the other known variables influencing the option price, and solving for the volatility.

Historical and implied volatility are used to forecast the future volatility of a currency. A problem arises however, because historical or implied volatility may not actually predict a currency's future volatility. One of the greatest risks to the option writer is an inaccurate forecast of volatility since this may cause a significant mispricing of an option.

INTEREST RATES

The time value of an option will change if interest rates change and all other variables remain constant, since a change in interest rates affects the forward foreign exchange rate.

For call options, time value increases when domestic interest rise and decreases when foreign interest rates rise.

For put options, time value decreases when domestic interest rates rise and increases when foreign interest rates rise.

Time value	Call	Put
Domestic rates increase	+	−
Foreign rates increase	−	+

Option pricing models

While it is possible to identify the major variables affecting the price of an option and to observe general boundary pricing conditions, it can be very difficult to determine the precise value of an option over time. In order to achieve this end, it is necessary to use option pricing models and the support of computer systems.

Option pricing models examine the variables described previously and derive the 'fair value' or price of the option. Option pricing models also quantify the impact of a change in any of these variables on the option price. It should be remembered that market conditions are not static and the variables influencing the price of an option can change at any time in a dynamic market-place.

The foundation of present day option pricing theory was published in 1973 by Fischer Black and Myron Scholes. Their work examined the pricing of options on stocks and developed a model which, given certain assumptions, derived an exact solution for the value of a European option when the underlying asset does not pay dividends. Subsequent option valuation models were adjusted for stocks paying dividends and physical commodities with associated carrying costs.

Mark Garman and Steven Kohlhaggen developed an option model to price European currency options. Their work takes into account the fact that a currency, unlike a stock where the forward date premium is equal to the riskless interest rate, may be at forward premium or discount depending on the interest rate differential. Garman and Kohlhaggen employ a constant dividend model to value a European currency option. In essence, the Garman–Kohlhaggen formulation is an amended Black–Scholes model which takes into account the currency market's spot and forward relationships which are driven by foreign and domestic interest rates.

To date, a closed form solution for the pricing of American style currency options has not been formulated. Because these options can be exercised at any time prior to expiration, interest rates have an impact on the option value which makes the price of an American option more difficult to quantify. While a European currency option is always priced off the forward rate, an American option may be priced off the spot or forward rate depending on the interest rate differential. It is the interest rate differential which determines the likelihood that an American option will be excercised early. To price American options, basic pricing models are usually combined with a form of numerical approximation to estimate the additional value of the American option.

While it is beyond the scope of this discussion to present an in-depth review of these option models several points should be raised.

The models reveal that when an option is priced at its fair value an equilibrium position exists such that a foreign exchange position can be established through a combination of borrowing and investment which in essence replicates the option. Through the hedge ratio, the option pricing models describe the correlation between the option price and the exchange rate at any point in time. By holding a cash position which is continually adjusted according to the hedge ratio, the profit and loss profile of the option can be replicated.

For example, with the sterling spot rate at $1.40, a sterling $1.40 call option may have a hedge ratio of .50. This means that for every $1.0 move in spot the options price will increase by $0.50. The immediate price behaviour of a call on £100,000 could be replicated by purchasing £50,000. For every change in the spot rate it would be necessary to adjust this cash holding. If the spot rate appreciated to $1.50 the option would be very deep in-the-money and the hedge ratio could be .98. At this point £98,000 should be held. If the spot rate declined to $1.35 the hedge ratio might be .30 and at this time only £30,000 would be held.

In a similar manner it is possible to replicate the behaviour of a cash foreign exchange position by adjusting an options position according to the hedge ratio. If the sterling spot rate were $1.35 and a sterling $1.40 call had a hedge ratio of .30 it would be necessary to buy 3.3 × sterling $1.40 calls for a change in the premium level of the option to equate to a given movement in the spot rate.

The importance of the hedge ratio cannot be overstated, for it is through the hedge ratio that market-makers in currency options are able to manage the exposures of their option books.

In addition to the hedge ratio which describes the relationship of the option price to cash foreign exchange rates, option pricing models derive correlations between an options price and changes in volatility, interest rates, and the passage of time.

All option pricing models are based on certain assumptions and to the extent that these assumptions accurately reflect actual market conditions, the option prices they formulate should be accurate valuations of an option's worth. However, these assumptions may not reflect actual market economic conditions, in which case the options prices will be inaccurate.

Even with inaccuracies it is important to point out that, despite inaccuracies, option pricing models are widely used by market-makers and professional traders in the market-place to achieve the following:

1. Calculate historical/implied volatility.
2. Establish what an options price should be.
3. Monitor pricing relationships between cash and options markets to ensure that boundary pricing conditions are not violated.
4. Evaluate trading and hedging strategies.
5. Manage risks associated with option positions.

Arbitrage in practice

A central feature of the relationship between the foreign exchange markets and currency options is that combinations of cash and options holdings can replicate one another. It has been shown that, at a given point in time, synthetic cash market positions can be created using options and that the behaviour of an option can be replicated by a cash position continually adjusted according to the hedge ratio.* In addition, a combination of a long foreign exchange position and a put can create a call, and a combination of a short foreign exchange position and a call can create a put. It is these equivalent positions that are the basis for the most important arbitrage relationships in the currency option markets.

Equivalence arbitrage, as it is sometimes called, involves the purchase and/or sale of combinations of options and cash foreign exchange positions when price disparities appear between the equivalent positions described previously. This arbitrage will be carried out when price anomalies make it possible to lock-in a profit between equivalent market positions.

Professional arbitrageurs and market-makers have developed computer programs which, given spot and forward rates, interest rates and the trader's volatility estimates, can calculate whether the prices of equivalent positions are in line with one another. These programs make it possible for the traders to monitor market prices continuously and to identify and take advantage of price disparities which may develop.

Equivalence arbitrage can be considered the most important arbitrage because it ensures that the prices between options and cash exchange rates are in line, and also maintains the relative prices of calls and puts. Even so, it is rare for anyone other than professional traders to be able to take advantage of equivalence arbitrage. Apart from the fact that the public cannot identify arbitrage opportunities and act on them as quickly as the professional trader, commission costs, margin requirements and bid-offer spreads significantly influence the profitability of such opportunities.

Other riskless arbitrage opportunities do develop from time to time. For example, a foreign exchange customer may call several banks and discover that there is a pricing disparity between the prices they are quoting for a particular option. Alternatively, two exchanges may show arbitrage prices for the same or similar options. Such arbitrages will be traded, and the market prices brought into line.

At times, riskless arbitrage opportunities can also develop between the over-the-counter (OTC) and exchange traded currency option markets. For instance, when a large currency option deal is transacted in the OTC market it can take time for the participants in the exchange market to find out that the demand for a particular option has increased and to adjust prices accordingly. This can lead to pricing disparities between the two markets which result in the possibility of a riskless arbitrage.

Riskless arbitrage will occur more frequently within or because of trading

---

* In practice, any such replication may be vulnerable to subsequent changes in the variables influencing the price of an option, e.g. volatility.

in the OTC market than in the exchange traded markets. This is largely due to the fact that information flows are more restricted in a 'private' than a public market-place. As the currency option market matures, information will be less restricted and riskless arbitrage opportunities will continue to decline.

Risk arbitrage, like riskless arbitrage, is based on identifying pricing anomalies within a market-place. Risk arbitrage, however, usually involves taking a position which will be profitable 'if something happens' or if an evaluation of a possible price misalignment proves to be correct. Certainly, it is fair to say there are times when it is quite difficult to distinguish between risk arbitrage and an outright speculative position.

An example of risk arbitrage would be as follows. Given that the Philadelphia Stock Exchange (PHLX) trades an American-style currency option and the Chicago Board Option Exchange (CBOE) trades a European style option, the spread between the prices of an option traded at each exchange could increase significantly. If an option valuation model were to determine that the CBOE option was underpriced and the PHLX option was overpriced, a trader could buy the CBOE option and sell the PHLX option. If the model's option valuation was correct the spread between these options should come back into line. This arbitrage is not riskless, however, since the profitability will be influenced by the following:

1. The accuracy of the model's option valuation.
2. The fact that the PHLX option can be exercised prior to expiration while the CBOE option cannot be exercised until the expiration date.

Another example would be using the estimated option values generated by a pricing model to discover if options on the same exchange were under- or overvalued and taking a position in the market based on this information. It might be that the sterling $1.40 calls were undervalued, and the $1.45 calls overvalued. A trader might buy the $1.40 calls and sell the $1.45 calls expecting the prices to come into line. The size of each option position would be established according to the hedge ratio to maintain neutrality with regard to the effect of short-term exchange rate movements. This arbitrage cannot be viewed as riskless because the accuracy of the model's output is not certain, and a large move in the foreign exchange rate would influence the neutrality of the position.

During the past two years, currency options have been sold into the financial markets in the form of warrants and in conjunction with other Eurobond issues. On a number of occasions an evaluation of the pricing of the instrument revealed an underlying currency option price which was not in line with expected values. Those who were in a position to purchase or sell the issues were able to carry out intermarket risk arbitrage trades.

An option position taken because of the view that a currency will be devalued or revalued can also be considered a risk arbitrage. This would be similar to a risk arbitrage carried out on a stock using options when the take-over of a company is believed possible.

While arbitrage relationships have a significant influence on the pricing and trading of options, the vast majority of trading within the currency options markets is a result of hedgers using the markets to manage foreign exchange exposures or currency option books, and traders trying to profit from a correct view of either currency direction or volatility forecasts. The profitable arbitrage opportunities which do develop are usually closed quickly by professional market-makers and arbitrageurs.

Option trading and hedging strategies

The most frequently employed option trading strategies are based upon either directional forecasts of the underlying exchange rate or views of the future volatility of the currency. Option writing is used in conjunction with directional and volatility trading, or in its own right as a means of enhancing income flows through the time decay of the option.

Note: Examples of trading strategies given in this section are based on the Philadelphia Stock Exchange American-style British Pound option of £12,500.

Option buying

Option buying is a commonly used directional strategy.* Traders are attracted by the leverage afforded by long option positions as well as the risk/reward profile of unlimited profit potential and limited risk. The key to successful option buying is to forecast correctly the price movement of the underlying currency during the life of the option. Descriptions of the purchase of calls and puts have already been presented yet it is also important to point out that care should be taken when selecting particular options in a buying strategy to ensure that the strike price and expiration date accurately reflect the currency outlook and expected timing of the exchange rate move.

Depending on the type and timing of an anticipated currency move, an option buyer should decide whether to purchase in-, at-, or out-of-the-money options. The final decision should be determined by the magnitude of the anticipated move and the aggressiveness of the trader. In-the-money options are the most sensitive to movements in the underlying spot rate. However, the cost of this option is greater than at-, or out-of-the-money options because it already holds intrinsic value. In-the-money options are often used by traders when a moderate price move is expected because of their close correlation to the cash prices.

The sensitivity of an at-the-money option to exchange rate movements is less than that of an in-the-money option, as is its cost. At-the-money options are usually purchased by traders who expect a price move but wish to reduce the initial cost of the option position.

Out-of-the-money options are considered appropriate for aggressive traders expecting sharp or rapid exchange rate movements. Although the initial cost of the option is less than for in- or at-the-money options, the underlying currency must make a substantial price move before the out-of-

---

* The following strategy evaluation is based on expiration analysis.

the-money option becomes valuable. However, due to the low initial cost of the option, the percentage return on an immediate sharp movement in the foreign exchange rate will be higher than for an in- or at-the-money option.

The expiration date of an option is also carefully considered by those initiating long option positions. Near month options will be more sensitive to exchange rate moves than far date options. Traders should select options with expiration dates which provide enough time for a price move to occur and at the same time react to the underlying currency movements.

Option spreads

Another means of taking a directional view of the market is through the purchase and sale of option spreads. A spread position involves buying one option and selling another of the same class (either calls or put) yet with different terms (strike price or expiration date). This strategy permits the spread buyer to profit from an expected price move yet reduces the cost of the initial position. The spread buyer is willing to forego unlimited profit potential and in doing so reduces the risk or cost of the strategy.

A vertical spread is established by buying and selling an option with the same expiration date but different strike prices. A horizontal spread involves buying and selling an option with the same strike price but different expiration dates. A diagonal spread is any combination of vertical and horizontal spreads. The options purchased and sold have different expiration dates as well as strike prices.

BULL CALL SPREAD

The option trader who establishes a bull call spread expects the underlying currency to appreciate. A moderate advance in prices is anticipated because if a large movement was forecast an outright call position would be established.

A bull call spread is a vertical spread which entails buying a call and selling another call with a higher strike price. The bull spread will outperform the outright purchase of a call if the currency advances slowly and moderately until expiration. If, however, there is a short-term move or a sustained larger upward move the return on a call position will be greater than that on the bull spread. The maximum profitability of this trade is the difference between the options' strike prices less the initial cost of the position.

Example

Buy 100 sterling or British pound $1.45 calls at $0.025		($31,250.00)
Sell 100 British pound $1.50 calls at	$0.01	$12,500.00
	Net cost – $0.0150	($18,750.00)

The P/L graph of this position at expiration is shown in Fig. 6.9.

A bull call spread is always a debit transaction because the call with the lower strike price must always trade for more than a call with a higher strike price if both options have the same expiration date.

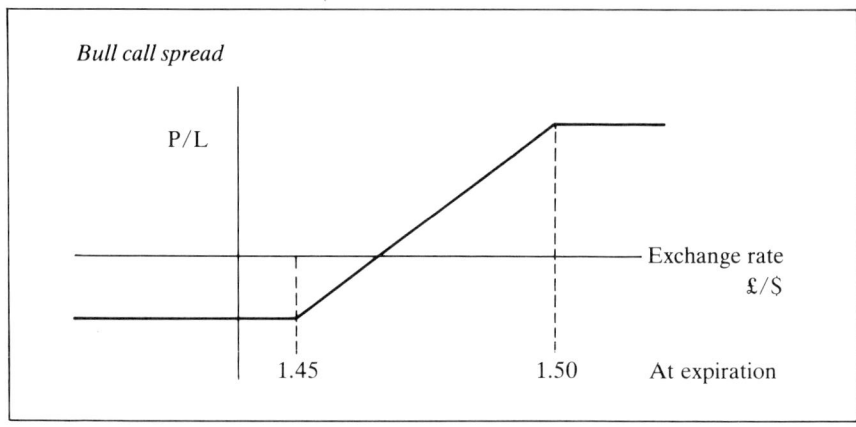

Fig. 6.9.

BEAR PUT SPREAD

An option trader who establishes a bear put spread expects a moderate decline in prices by the time the option expires. If a rapid downward price move is expected an outright put purchase would be a better strategy to initiate. A bear put spread can outperform the outright purchase of a put if the currency declines slowly and moderately by expiration.

The bear put spread is a vertical spread which entails buying a put and selling another put with a lower strike price. The profit potential of this spread is limited to the difference between the strike prices less the initial cost of the position. The maximum risk of a bear put spread is the initial premium cost.

Buy 100 sterling or British pound $1.45 puts at $0.020		($25,000.00)
Sell 100 British pound $1.40 puts at	$0.008	$10,000.00
	Net cost – $0.012	($15,000.00)

A P/L profile of this position at expiration is shown in Fig. 6.10.

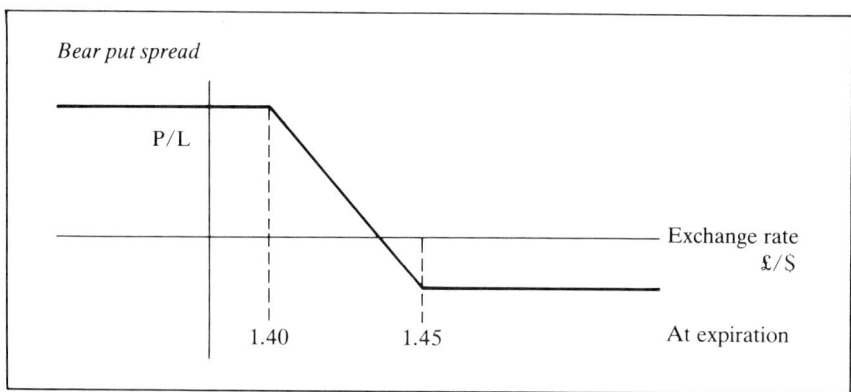

Fig. 6.10

SELLER OF A VERTICAL SPREAD

The seller of a vertical spread initiates the trade with a different currency forecast trading objective than the spread buyer. The spread seller will receive a premium which will be retained if the currency moves against the view of the call buyer. If, however, the spread seller's forecast is incorrect, the maximum loss of the position is limited to the difference between the strike price less the initial premium received.

CALENDAR SPREADS

The trader initiating a calendar spread sells an option and buys another with the same strike price and a more distant expiration date. The trader expects a profit from the fact that the time value premium of the near-term option disappears more rapidly than that of the longer-date option. Rather than profiting from a correct prediction of the direction of the underlying currency, the trader is selling time value. If the currency remains relatively stable until the near-term option expires, the neutral calendar spread will be profitable.

The maximum profit of this position is unlimited if the long position is not offset at the expiration of the short position. The maximum loss is the cost of establishing the position, since the longer term option will always be worth more than the near-term option.

The calendar spread is graphically represented in Fig. 6.11.

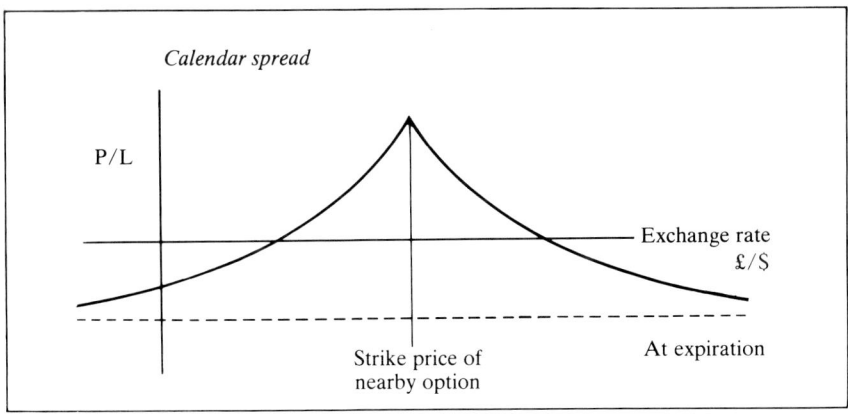

Fig. 6.11.

Ratios/Weighting

Option strategies can be made more or less aggressive, depending upon the number of options and the strike price of the options written relative to the purchased options or to a cash position. The following list gives examples of this:

1. Buy outright call – this is aggressively bullish.

2. Buy call with lower strike price, sell call with higher strike price – this is less aggressively bullish.
3. Buy call with lower strike price, sell two calls with higher strike price – this may be bullish, bearish or a neutral strategy, depending upon the specific strike prices purchased and sold.

Selling options

The selling of an option may be carried out in conjunction with long options, cash positions or as a strategy in its own right. The sale of options against long option positions has already been discussed. Another important selling strategy is referred to as covered writing.

COVERED OPTION WRITING

An option writer who calls the currency against which a call or put is written is referred to as a 'covered writer'. A covered option seller receives the premium and assumes the obligation to either purchase or deliver currency if the option is exercised.

If the exchange rate does not change during the life of the option, an out-of-the-money option will expire worthless and the option writer profits from the initial premium received.

In the event of a sharp movement of the currency, it is possible that the option holder will exercise the option to buy or sell currency at what would be a 'better-than-market' rate.

Whilst the option holder gains directly from the foreign exchange rate movement, the option writer's gain is the initial premium paid plus the difference between the exchange rate and the strike price when the option was initially sold. The option writer receives the premium now and is willing to forego potential additional profit in the future.

UNCOVERED OPTION WRITING

An option seller who does not own the asset against which a call or put is written is called an uncovered or naked writer. The uncovered option writer receives a premium and is obliged to purchase or deliver currency at the option holder's request. The option writer's maximum profit is the initial premium received, whilst his maximum loss is unlimited.

Option hedging

It is important to remember that the initial development of the currency option market was largely a result of foreign exchange hedgers' needs for a new exchange rate management tool. Options provide those exposed to exchange rate movements with the right to transfer exchange rate risk when it is needed. The decision regarding whether to hedge an exchange rate exposure, and what type of hedge to establish if needed, is generally based upon an evaluation of objectives and risk parameters, cost sensitivity and the currency outlook of those responsible for the management of a foreign exchange exposure or position.

If a foreign exchange exposure is not hedged, the underlying asset value will fluctuate with movements in the spot. A forward hedge will lock-in a fixed rate that will protect the asset value against adverse exchange rate moves, but at the same time will eliminate the possibility of benefiting from favourable exchange rate moves. An option hedge locks-in a rate that will protect an asset's value against adverse exchange rate movements, yet at the same time, for the cost of the premium, retains the possibility of benefiting from favourable exchange rate movements.

Conclusion

The development of the currency options market during the past five years reflects growing interest in this instrument. It is clear that currency options have attracted the attention of professionals in the foreign exchange and options markets.

This overview should serve as an introduction to currency options for those involved in the management of foreign exchange exposures and traders who wish to participate in this market. Potential users of currency options should become familiar with option pricing, be aware of the role and influence of arbitrage relationships on the pricing and trading of options and study the many uses of this new instrument. It is through this educational process that the new dimensions which currency options bring to foreign exchange management and trading can be understood and the benefits of this instrument fully realised.

CHAPTER 7

Interest rate and currency swaps

Martin Bralsford

The term 'swap' has become commonplace in the financial jargon of the 1980s, and swaps look like remaining a central element of the financial engineer's toolkit for many years yet. We are all familiar with the concept of swapping, probably from our schooldays, and yet swaps are sometimes talked of as though they were an instrument of some black art.

At the most basic level, the simple act of borrowing and repaying money is a swap. Current purchasing power has been swapped for future purchasing power at an agreed price: the nominal interest rate. Equally, outright foreign exchange transactions in the cash markets are swaps – so many dollars are swapped for so many Deutschmarks on an agreed settlement date. Yet neither of these transactions is a swap in the sense that the word is used nowadays in the financial markets.

'Swap' is a generic term for a self-liquidating transaction between two entities (which does not create current purchasing power in the hands of either), whereby each is obliged to make a series of payments to the other over an agreed period of time, which are estimated at the outset to have an equivalent present value when discounted at the respective cost of funds in the relevant primary financial markets.

Clearly the transaction only has a purpose if the series of future payments is not identical with respect to either timing or variability of amounts to be paid. For interest swaps, the reference points are usually market rates of interest and for currency swaps, market exchange rates. Of course, the two may be combined into one transaction to result in a cross-currency interest rate swap.

What could be the driving force behind the growth in swaps and why should each counterparty find a swap attractive? Swaps do not, of themselves, raise funds. On completion of the documentation of most swaps, neither counterparty has created spendable funds for itself. The swap has not financed the acquisition of assets by one party and it has not provided a home for surplus cash for another. Swaps have the quality of the Cheshire cat's smile. Their value lies in arbitrage, in the broad sense of the word. The strict definintion of arbitrage – riskless profit – should not be used in connection with swaps. They do involve a risk as to credit exposure, but no market risk. The risk is essentially a long-term settlement risk and few transactions can be completed without incurring this type of risk. The sources of the arbitrage are the primary credit markets and swaps provide the bridges between them. The mid 1980s have seen the trend towards global capital markets confirmed. Borrowers are learning to access the full range of national and international credit markets in seeking the most cost-effective funds. Investors and lenders of funds are similarly combing world markets for the most favourable risk/reward relationship. If global markets become a reality, then some decline in swap activity could be foreseen. However, the harmonisation of prospectus legislation, liberalisation of exchange controls, neutrality of tax legislation, reduction in minimum size of transactions and the disappearance of xenophobic attitudes still appear to be far away. All of these factors, and many more, serve to clog the free flow of credit which creates the conditions under which a global equilibrium in market prices will not occur naturally. Schemes to relieve the pressure that such blockages create give rise to profit opportunities: arbitrage. As in the physical sciences, inequality is the source of all local movement. Giving effect to the forces at work in achieving equilibrium between financial markets is the purpose of swaps. The necessary condition for a market in swaps to develop is the blockage of the flow of funds that might otherwise be expected, which in turn creates an unnatural price differential between markets. The swap market is the relief valve.

Distinguishing the swap agreement from a straightforward gamble has exercised the ingenuity of lawyers. Gaming contracts are not enforceable through the courts, under English law at least, and the swap agreement appears to bear close resemblance to a bet on the likelihood of an uncertain future event, which, if it occurred, would give rise to a settlement in favour of one party. Given the appropriate motivation, lawyers have shown the way forward, in associating swaps with contracts of insurance and loan agreements so that, although the matter remains largely untested in the courts, participants in the market are confident of the validity of the commitments given and received. When a swap is not connected with hedging some other exposure, the swap may be regarded as a straightforward speculation to which the attitude of English law is not at all certain.

Development of the market

Without wishing to provoke any unproductive arguments over the genesis of the swap markets, one starting point is London in the early 1970s. Many UK companies wished to expand overseas and were restricted by exchange controls as to how such direct investment could be funded. Equally, investment fund managers wished to diversify their portfolio into foreign securities and were inhibited by similar restrictions. Both had access to spendable funds in domestic sterling which could not be used to purchase the required foreign currency for investment at official exchange rates. They were forced to borrow currencies in the international markets and use these proceeds for overseas investment instead of their domestic sterling. In a regime accustomed to fixed exchange rates and before the arrival of the volatile markets in the wake of the 1973 oil crisis, matching currency assets and liabilities did not seem quite so obvious to many practitioners then, as it does now after more than a decade of violent changes in the currency markets!

The same exchange controls also restricted foreign-controlled companies from funding themselves in the domestic sterling markets above certain levels. The market in offshore sterling was thin and relatively expensive, being very well insulated from the domestic market.

Thus, the back-to-back and parallel loans were created. In the simplest form of back-to-back loan, the holder of domestic sterling would place it on deposit with a bank in London and borrow, say, its dollar equivalent from that bank. Banks were not so sensitive to their balance sheet totals in those days and, given that satisfactory set-off rights were granted, could afford to reduce the spread between borrowing and lending interest rates. The parallel loan took the process a stage further by having a UK parent company lend domestic sterling to a foreign-controlled company in the United Kingdom in return for the foreign parent company lending currency to the foreign subsidiary of the UK parent. All payments of interest and repayments of principal were made conditional on equivalent amounts being received from the counterparty. In so doing, bankers' spreads were eliminated as the bankers' role in the transaction was reduced to that of an arranger, for which they charged a fee.

It became apparent to all concerned that the economic effect of the parallel loan could be obtained without the need for borrowing and lending but by each party agreeing to make a net payment to the other calculated by reference to an agreed formula. Such an agreement is the essence of the swap and these became evident in the latter part of the 1970s.

The early parallel loans tended to be at fixed interest rates with the differential being determined by supply and demand in that market. Each potential participant would compare the interest differential on the parallel loan with its cost of funds in the primary markets for each component and almost invariably the parallel loan proved more effective. Taking the example of a cash-rich UK participant, it could invest surplus sterling in UK gilt-edged securities and borrow at a margin of, say, 50 basis point over the equivalent risk-free rate in currency. This position was the mirror image of the foreign participant, which would also lose 50 basis points by being on opposite sides of the respective markets. In addition, the domestic markets of one participant may not have been freely available to the other, which could lead to further increases in overall funding costs. Instead of losing 1% ($3\frac{1}{2} - 2\frac{1}{2}$) on the overall position, the US company could agree to lend $2 million to the UK company for ten years on the condition that reciprocal loan of £1 million was made. The US company would pay a net amount of 3% of £1 million (£30,000) to the UK company at the end of each year, and both would be £5,000 per annum better off. Provided effective set-off rights are established there is no credit risk as long as exchange rates and interest rates stay in the same relationship as at the outset.

Example

	UK company		US company	
	Amount	Cost/Return %	Amount	Cost/Return %
Yield on 10-year government securities	£1m	10	$2m	7
Cost of 10-year fixed rate borrowing	$2m	$7\frac{1}{2}$	£1m	$10\frac{1}{2}$
Net funding position	nil	$2\frac{1}{2}$	nil	$3\frac{1}{2}$
Net interest receipt (payment)	£25,000 p.a.		£35,000 p.a.	

Of course, exchange rates could not be expected to remain constant and parallel loan agreements soon included top-up clauses, which required the currency amounts to be brought back to equivalence from time to time. This was achieved by requiring the participant which had become the net debtor either to advance an additional amount to the other or repay an appropriate part of the loan. The decision as to which course was selected would be determined by the relevant cost of funds at the time of the adjustment.

From these rudimentary types of transaction developed more sophisticated parallel loan arrangements in which banks took part as a principal rather than as arranger. This was probably a function of the increasingly demanding requirements of non-bank participants to avoid tax problems, credit risks and timing mismatches.

In general, the early 1980s saw the liberalisation of exchange controls and removal of taxation constraints on the free flow of capital. It could reasonably have been expected that the need for parallel loans and their derivative swaps would subside. Two factors served to increase the need for swaps to transform the type of funds supplied into that demanded.

First, the liberalisation of financial markets around the world widened the range of credit sources available to international borrowers. An ever-increasing number of borrowers can use the capital markets of the United States, Japan, the United Kingdom, Germany and Switzerland. Yet each market retains its own character. Some prefer sovereign credits, some prefer issuers that have recognised credit ratings, some are attracted by well-known brand names, some are attracted to high-coupon currency issues, some like US issuers, others do not; the idiosyncracies are numerous. It is often not the case that the requirements of potential borrowers and investors coincide. For instance, a large US corporate issuer may be able to raise fixed rate Swiss francs on very fine terms as a result of the strong attraction of investors to names like IBM, Ford, etc. On the other hand, a less well-known but nevertheless strong credit with an A1+/P1 credit rating could raise floating rate US dollars cheaply in the US Commercial Paper market. The latter may be happy to swap with, say, Ford and receive interest rate in US dollars at slightly less than it pays on its US Commerical Paper in order to obtain the Swiss franc liability at a much more attractive rate than it could through a direct issue in the Swiss franc market. Ford could obtain very cheap US dollars.

Example

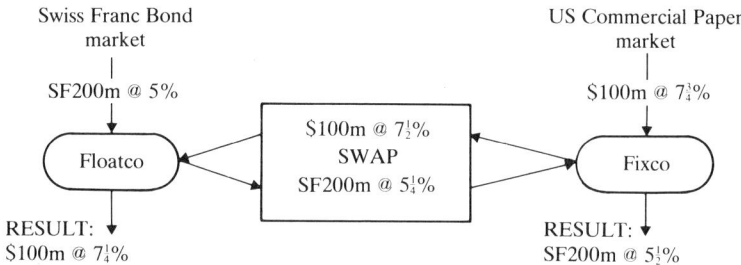

If Fixco could obtain Swiss francs at 5.75% as a direct issue, then it has saved 25 basis points by using the US Commercial Paper market as its source of credit and the swap to achieve the type of funds it wanted, i.e. fixed-rate Swiss francs. On the other hand, Floatco has effectively raised $100 million at 50 basis points less than the A1+/P1 rate in that market. Both parties have achieved the required amount of funding of the required specification at a lower rate than either could have by direct issues in each market. The overall saving is a function of the arbitrage gain resulting from investor preferences as to type of borrower in each market. The split of the saving between Fixco and Floatco is partly a function of supply and demand and partly their respective view of the other's ability to meet its obligation under the swap.

A second stimulus to the swap market is that investors have preferred the credit risk of prime industrial and commercial entities rather than banks. In the 1970s, banks were regarded as first-class credit risks and investors believed that deposits placed with banks were not at risk. Following several bank failures and the high level of bank exposure to poor-quality sovereign credits, perhaps due to the re-cycling of oil price induced trade imbalances in the 1980s, investors came to prefer corporate sector risk. Thus at the same time as the authorities were opening their borders to the free flow of capital and allowing foreign borrowers in, so investors wished to diversify their lending directly on their own account rather than indirectly through banks. Consequently, borrowers could obtain much more attractive funding in the world capital markets than from banks, and the yield gap arising from differing investor preferences in each of the various capital markets became exaggerated.

Investment and merchant banks were quick to realise the opportunities inherent in these trends. As they had never been major providers of credit and takers of deposits, the role of arranger came naturally to them. They were experienced in underwriting and distributing securities through the capital markets in return for fee income. Attaching swaps to the range of services already provided was quite natural. By 1985 most commercial banks had developed a swap capability and it had become fair to say that an active market had developed in the major categories of swap. Instead of the bespoke transactions of a decade ago, swap terms were now being quoted on the usual information services (e.g. Reuters), brokers were active in matching market positions and standard terms and conditions were becoming accepted. For certain categories of swap, an active secondary market has come about and corporate treasurers can now manage their liability portfolio as actively as any bank, marking to market each liability and being held to account for opportunities foregone.

Types of swap

Swaps can be categorised in a number of ways:

1. Interest rate swaps – fixed rate against floating rate, floating rate basis.
2. Currency swaps – constant exchange rate, variable exchange rate.
3. Interest rate and currency swaps – any combination of (1) and (2) above.
4. Differential swaps – swaps involving a net payment from one party to the other at the outset.

1. *Interest rate swaps*

Most swaps involve streams of payment computed by reference to different market rates of interest. There are a number of standard reference rates which are selected as those being readily observable, objectively defined and requiring no subjective interpretation. For example:

- Yield on UK gilt-edged stock of the required maturity (fixed)
- Yield on US Treasury Bond of required maturity (fixed)
- London Inter-Bank Offered Rate (LIBOR) as quoted by specified reference banks (floating)
- US Commercial Paper discount rate as published by the Federal Reserve (Form H15) for a specified maturity (floating)
- Prime rate or base lending rates as announced by specified banks (floating)
- US Bankers' Acceptance (floating)
- US Treasury Bills (floating)

The above shows some standard reference interest rates for interest rate swaps in sterling and US dollars. The typical swap is fixed against floating and has an overall swap life of between two and ten years, with most transactions between three and seven years. The usual practice is for the floating rate element to be quoted at LIBOR (or maybe 1% below LIBOR) and then the fixed rate element to vary according to market conditions and be quoted as so many basis points over the reference fixed interest yield, e.g. 40 basis points over the seven-year gilt-edged yield.

It is helpful to have interest rate swaps quoted to a standard format to facilitate ease of comparison and secondary market pricing.

Although it is theoretically possible to create an interest rate swap with the interest period on one element being any integral multiple of the longer interest period, in fixed against floating swaps it is customary for the floating element to be three-month (90-day) or six-month (180-day) interest periods.

The floating against floating swap is where the interest periods on each element have the same duration. The purpose of the swap is to crystallise the

Arbitrage

interest differential between two parallel short-term money markets. A common variant of a floating against floating swap is US Commercial Paper against US dollar LIBOR for 30-day interest periods. The differential between the US Commercial Paper and US dollar LIBOR fluctuates quite significantly and many participants in these markets like to have certainty over a period of several years before committing to a particular funding or investment alternative. Lenders often prefer to do so at a margin over whatever interest rate they pay for the major part of their own funding. If they fund themselves in the inter-bank market, then they will wish to lend at a margin over inter-bank rates. Lending at a margin over some other reference rate may give cause for a higher margin to allow for risk. By using a floating against floating swap, the risk can be reduced to a reasonable certainty.

2. *Currency swaps*

The simplest is the variable exchange rate currency swap where the counterparties agree to exchange currency amounts with immediate settlement and then re-exchange the same amount in one currency for a changed amount of the second at some pre-determined future date.

This type of currency swap takes place regularly in the foreign exchange market and saves dealing costs compared with an initial sale/purchase followed by a second and opposite forward transaction. The adjustment to the rate at which currencies are first exchanged to that implicit in the re-exchange depends on the interest differential between the respective currencies over the life of the transaction, established at the outset.

An alternative is the constant exchange rate currency swap, under which identical amounts of currency are exchanged by the counterparties to be re-exchanged in exactly the same amounts at an agreed future date. In consideration of what are effectively collateral loans in each currency, both counterparties make payments to the other. These payments may be made in the currency of the respective loan or they may be netted against each other at a pre-determined exchange rate. Depending on which method is chosen, the result could be quite different when measured in either currency.

The tripartite relationship between current exchange rates, future exchange rates and interest rates is well established in the financial markets and gives rise to one of the earliest arbitrage opportunities (which is dealt with elsewhere in this book and will not be expanded upon here).

3. *Interest rate and currency swaps*

Such swaps are clearly the most complex and usually give rise to the most significant benefits to the participants.

The cross-currency 'fixed against fixed', 'floating against floating' and 'floating against fixed' are attractive to counterparties who have access to relatively low-cost funds in one currency but do not require a liability in that currency. By means of one of the above swaps they can create the desired type of liability in another currency. Looked at another way, an investor may know of a relatively high-yielding investment opportunity in which the returns do not match the criteria against which performance is assessed as regards currency and exposure to movements in interest rates. A swap will enable the investor to capture the extra yield whilst meeting the standard investment criteria.

It must be recalled when establishing the optimum method of procuring funds with particular characteristics that the swap does not create the funds. If the arbitrage condition is to be adhered to as closely as possible, like must be compared with like. The possibility of borrowing short and entering into a long-term fixed against floating swap does not create long-term funding. There is a considerable temptation to compare, say, the cost of a long-term bond issue in sterling against the all-in cost of short-term US dollar Commercial Paper plus a floating US dollar against fixed sterling swap. However, the cost of a committed facility of equivalent term to that of the bond issue must also be taken into account. For this reason, underwritten note issuance facilities often prove an attractive source of credit as they carry a low-cost, long-term commitment to provide funds. As floating rate US dollars are almost always marketable as one element of a cross-currency floating against fixed swap, a note issuance facility in conjunction with such a swap is often the lowest-cost means of creating fixed rate term funding.

4. *Differential swaps*

Most swaps commence on such terms that the two streams of future payments have equivalent present values. However, it is possible to structure swaps so that the streams do not have equivalent present values and therefore an initial cash payment is made by the recipient of the higher value future payment stream. Structuring swaps along these lines is usually dictated by the considerations which will be specific to the individual circumstances, especially taxation issues. However, the larger the initial payment, the greater the ensuing credit exposure incurred by its payer.

Financial evaluation of swaps

The most appropriate technique for evaluating a swap is the net present value of its cash flows. It is dangerous to work by comparison of stated yields, interest rates and interest rate differentials. The quoted yields in the underlying financial markets, to which returns under swaps relate, are calculated according to a wide variety of conventions as regards the following:

1. Frequency of interest payments and compounding effect.
2. Calculation of elapsed time – actual days, notional 30-day months, 360- or 365-day year.
3. Interest paid in advance (discount) or in arrears.
4. Timing of deemed principal repayments being applied in reduction of interest-bearing balance.
5. Interest payments made gross or net of withholding taxes and consequent cash flow impact.

Arbitrage

The evaluation of the swap requires the exhaustive inquiry into all aspects of how the actual stream of payments and receipts will be computed. Furthermore, in fixed against floating swaps, either same or cross-currency, the remittances arising under the floating component will change over time. One approach is to forecast the floating rate remittances, net them off against their fixed rate counterparts and discount the difference back to a present value using the relevant interest rate for the maturity of each net remittance. This would be relevant if the swap is entered into as a standalone transaction and is viewed essentially as a speculation on movements in market rates.

If the swap is viewed as part of an overall arbitrage transaction which is expected to produce a more attractive result than an alternative direct transaction in the markets, then one of the remittance streams will be hedged against an almost equal and opposite remittance in the primary market. It is safer to evaluate each part of the swap in isolation if it is regarded as part of a composite transaction.

Let us assume that Newco wishes to raise £10 million of ten-year fixed rate sterling. It has two courses of action available:

1. It issues a Eurobond with an $11\frac{1}{2}\%$ coupon, paid annually in arrears, and bears issue expenses and commissions of 2% of the proceeds.
2. It has a ten-year committed source of six-month maturity US dollars at 40 basis points under LIBOR and an annual commitment fee of 12.5 basis points for ten years, paid semi-annually. It has been offered a swap under which it will pay $11\frac{1}{2}\%$ per annum semi-annually on £10 million for ten years and receive six-month US dollar LIBOR on the US dollar equivalent of £10 million at the outset of the swap, when £1=$1.50.

Looking at alternative (2), it can be seen that if it borrowed $15 million and sold it spot for sterling, it would realise £10 million. If it entered into a swap, it would receive a net amount of 27.5 basis points paid semi-annually on $15 million. Its value in sterling would depend on the exchange rate from time to time unless the US dollar receipts could be sold forward.

The first question is should Newco attribute the net income from the US dollars to the swap? Presumably it could have placed the proceeds of borrowing on deposit, perhaps at the bid rate, but nevertheless at above their cost. Strictly, only the spread between bid and offered rates of, say, 10 basis points, can be attributed to the swap. There is no exchange risk on the principal component as Newco will receive $15 million at the end of ten years in exchange for £10 million with which it can repay the dollar advance.

Newco's calculations show that the equivalent cost of funds under the first alternative is 11.85% per annum compounded annually and that this is equivalent to 11.52% per annum compounded semi-annually.

So the present value of the sterling payments under the swap discounted at 11.52% is £9,9883 million, that is, £11,700 less than the actual initial receipt. In addition, the present value of the 10 basis points' income on $15 million should be calculated using the spot exchange rate of £1=$1.50 and discounted at 11.52%. The present value is £58,500. The combined value of the swap is £70,200, derived mainly from the attributed saving on the US dollars. This is the true arbitrage profit as it is subject only to settlement risk, but over a ten-year period, and assumes that forward cover of the net dollar inflow was obtained at the implicit interest differential.

Note that if an arrangement fee of $\frac{1}{2}\%$ flat was charged at the outset, the present value is reduced by £50,000 and the decision on which course to select is quite close run.

Credit risk in swaps

In evaluating swaps in terms of present value, some valuable insights into the credit risks are obtained. By repeating the exercise from time to time with respect to the remaining payments and receipts and using currently achievable interest rates and market exchange rates, the resulting present value, if positive, represents the credit exposure. This could be a material amount if the swap is a cross-currency, fixed against floating type with several years still to run. It is also possible that both counterparties could regard themselves as exposed to the other, but this is hardly likely to be a practical problem.

The key to credit exposure is in ensuring that the swap agreement makes all future payments and receipts conditional upon each other. This limits the amount of credit exposure, particularly as to principal amounts where the agreement is constituted as a parallel loan.

Some of the regulatory authorities are concerned that the credit exposures inherent in swaps are not properly reported in financial statements, particularly those for banks which are major players in the swap market.

Legal, accounting and tax issues

Legal

The documentation of a swap is gradually becoming more standardised, especially for the types of swap in which there is a high volume of activity, for example, fixed against floating and floating against floating US dollar transactions. The International Swap Dealers Associations Inc. has published a Code of Standard Wording, Assumptions and Provisions for Swaps. This applies to US dollar swaps but it is intended that future versions will deal with cross-currency swaps where the counterparties may be in different jurisdictions. The British Bankers Association has also published standard terms and conditions for swap transactions. These codes are useful in that they may be incorporated in swap documentation by reference and cover a vast number of fairly uncontentious points without the need for line-by-line drafting. A key aspect has been to make sure the swap contract steers well clear of being construed as a wager. Some of the early simple form swaps, where the parties agree to settle cash differences only, look very much like a wager. The closer the swap agreement either follows a parallel loan format or resembles a contract of insurance, the better. The latter may be fairly easy when the swap is connected with a specific issue of securities in the capital markets. For the time being, swaps remain in the class of financial transactions for which specific legal advice should be taken each time. Perhaps in the later 1980s this may cease to be the case and market custom and practice will have become so well established that the courts will accept it as such, but that remains to be seen.

To enable swaps to be unwound it is important that the contract should be assignable. The contentious point is the definition of an acceptable assignee, as it is impractical to specify names. For a variety of reasons, one counterparty may not be able to accept exposure to a substitute, even when of first-class credit.

Accounting

Most swaps are long-term transactions and will subsist across several balance sheet dates. As the various cash flows arising under a swap may not conform with the accrual concept of accounting, it is necessary to devise an accounting policy as to the apportionment of the cash flows which is consistent with generally accepted accounting principles. The first stage is to examine the motive for entering into the swap. If it is unconnected with any underlying financing transaction, then a fairly straightforward approach can be adopted, especially if the swap is not cross-currency. The payments and receipts have merely to be apportioned as to time and the appropriate fraction of the net amount taken to profit and loss. Only if the counterparty is in the business of trading swaps and intends to trade the swap could it be considered appropriate to value the swap as at the balance sheet date and take any difference from its previous carrying value to profit and loss. Such a practice is easier to defend on swaps for which there is an active market and firm prices to support the valuation. Also, it depends on the benefit of the swap actually being capable of being transferred.

On a cross-currency swap unconnected with hedging a currency asset or liability, movements in translation from time to time should be taken to profit and loss.

It is more common for swaps to be arranged as a hedge of another asset or liability carried in the balance sheet. Where this is the case, then it is necessary to look at the economic substance of combined position. If a company had issued a Swiss franc bond and hedged it with a fixed Swiss franc against a fixed US dollar swap of matching amount and maturity, then the substance is that the company has raised fixed rate US dollars. The accounting treatment should then follow the line it would have taken if US dollars had been raised directly. The only problem arises where the swap counterparty appears to be unlikely to be able to meet its commitment. If so, and the Swiss franc has strengthened, it may be necessary for the company to provide for the loss likely when the Swiss franc bond becomes due for repayment. This provision would be calculated with reference to spot exchange rates and almost certainly be charged to profit and loss rather than reserves as it could not be attributed to any other movements which may have arisen on other currency asset positions.

Companies are required to set out details of their loan capital as a note to the balance sheet. In the above example, it would be inappropriate to report the Swiss franc bond without also noting the collateral swap. This seems to be called for not just to comply with the true and fair view, but also a contingent liability may have arisen under the swap and this is required to be reported upon in any event. Presumably the purpose of reporting details of loan capital is so that shareholders and analysts have a view of the interest rate and currency exposures of the company. If swaps were not reported, the accounts could give a completely different picture from reality.

Tax

The tax problems on interest rate swaps are not too severe. Provided the swap is arranged with a recognised bank in the United Kingdom, there is no requirement to deduct withholding tax on the deemed interest flows and they may be settled in a net amount. If the swap is sold and a gain or loss realised, it is most likely that it will be taxed as though it was a capital gain or loss, unless the taxpayer trades in swaps. This may or may not be attractive to the taxpayer. If the swap had been hedging an issue in the capital market, it may be that the equivalent loss or gain on extinguishing that liability, whether or not realised, does not fall within the charge to tax. It is quite possible that a perfect hedge at the pre-tax level may not have the same result post-tax. To mitigate such effects it is possible that by locating the fund-raising and swapping activity in a subsidiary which has a financing trade, the pre- and post-tax hedge is maintained. All gains, losses, income and expenditure flows relating to the financing trade will be taxed as income of the trade. This ensures the symmetry of treatment sought in hedging transactions. Nevertheless, there are myriads of tax management opportunities in arranging swaps and swap-related financing, and it remains an area where specialist advice is always essential.

Where swaps include a cross-currency element, then the tax position becomes much more complex. Detailed discussion of the approach of the Inland Revenue is well beyond the scope of this book. Taxation of cross-currency swaps is an area on which tax specialists cannot always give advice confidently. It is recommended that they are consulted at an early stage in the timetable for completion of the swap as there are pre-emptive measures that can be incorporated which have no commercial effect but do simplify the tax position. Generally, tax practitioners prefer cross-currency swaps to be structured as parallel loans as the taxation consequences are more certain.

If the counterparty to a swap is not a UK-recognised bank, then it is usual for the Inland Revenue to require withholding tax to be deducted from any gross amounts paid by UK tax residents. This can destroy the economics of the swap for a foreign counterparty.

Swaps and the corporate treasurer

Until quite recently, corporate management concentrated its balance sheet management efforts almost exclusively upon fixed assets and net working capital. The long-term liabilities, such as loan capital, were managed in a fairly passive style. Funds were raised in the capital markets or in bank loans, depending on which were more attractive at the time the requirement arose. Once the funding exercise was complete, it was left alone for its entire life unless a fairly major reorganisation of the business took place. The capability for corporate treasurers to transform the structure of the loan portfolio by using swaps has changed all that. At one time it was possible for the treasurer to claim that there was little to be done if the company's view on interest rates changed and it has felt appropriate to carry less of its debt at fixed interest rates. Now, through use of the swap market, the treasurer can invariably take action to achieve the required interest rate profile. The debt portfolio can be marked to market just as though there were an active and liquid secondary market in each of its debts. This makes the treasurer's role that much more active. It is now possible to crystallise unrealised gains from earlier funding activities that have proved beneficial and not see the gain subsequently eroded as the movement in market rates reverses.

Such activities in swaps do not overload the balance sheet with too much debt and consequent surplus liquid funds, as the swap is not a fund-raising medium. The treasurer may turn over the debt portfolio as often as necessary and need only have regard to the creditworthiness of the swap counterparties.

Furthermore, swap transactions can be arranged at fairly short notice without the need for prospectus documentation typically required in a capital market issue. There are relatively brief windows in the corporate calendar when certain types of issue may be conveniently executed in the public markets. Swaps can be done much more readily as they call for less publicity and less assistance from other corporate staff functions.

The critical mass for a swap transaction is usually well below that for a capital market issue. This makes it possible for the treasurer to reach funding objectives with transactions for smaller amounts. For those of us who prefer to try to obtain averages of market rates over time, rather than go for broke on picking winners with a few blockbuster transactions, the swap is the ideal approach.

The same sort of arguments apply to the converse, where treasurers are managing hard core surplus liquidity. Rather than churning the investment portfolio, it may prove cheaper to shift the profile through the use of swaps. This may enable the funds to be kept in highly liquid, risk-free instruments, such as US dollar Treasury Bills, and yet obtain long-term yields and also different currency exposure through the appropriate swap.

Swaps have made the treasurer's job more interesting but excuses for missing opportunities will come less easily than before.

Outlook

It appears that the swap market should run and run. The potential demand for swaps is massive as managers become more accustomed to managing their financial position more actively. Even if swaps were limited to those related to transforming capital market issues, the market could be enormous, as one issue could lead to a cascade of swaps over its entire life as participants' views changed. On top of this could be layered the speculative demand, where participants are just taking a view on movements in interest or exchange rates and seek profit from what they hope is their foresight. If we examine other financial markets, we observe that volume of overall activity bears little relation to the end users' requirements. The turnover of the gilt-edged market is massive in relation to the government funding requirement. Equally, the foreign exchange market turnover is estimated at over twenty times the volume of world trade. The comparisons may not be entirely fair but do serve to indicate that the potential level of activity in any market exceeds that which may have been expected a priori.

Provided transaction expense is kept low, the swap market will attain massive volumes. Already the standardised transaction has reduced arrangement fees from 50 basis points or so on long-term transactions to negligible amounts.

It is difficult to see what might bring a stop to this market. If world capital markets become fully integrated, then it may reduce some of the demand for primary hedging swaps as end users of funds can more readily fund themselves directly in the cheapest market. There is also a chance that the regulatory authorities in the major financial centres may attempt to control the market. If banks' swap positions were to be restricted to a multiple of primary capital or some similar prudent control, then market growth could be stunted. But if the market is not restricted in this way and regulates itself so as to maintain a good record on defaults and standards of conduct, then it should become a permanent feature of the financial scenery.

CHAPTER 8

Cross-market arbitrage

John Heywood

Simple cash against forwards arbitrage

This chapter considers some of the ways in which the cash, short paper, Forex, futures and options markets may be arbitraged against each other. In order to provide a general context for the discussion all these markets are shown as alternative ways of approaching the classic cash against forwards arbitrage, here set out in its simplest form. These types of arbitrage – bills against futures, options against forward, and so on – are all forms of cross-market arbitrage in that they provide a price transfer mechanism across markets that are otherwise quite separate.

The basic principles are perhaps most easily understood by considering the situation of a man with £1 sterling who is deciding whether to invest it in sterling or Deutschmarks. We assume that the spot rate between Deutschmarks and sterling is 4.2650. Any citizen of the United Kingdom is perfectly free to choose between holding £1 or converting it into DM4.2650. We will assume that at current interest rates he is able to obtain $12\frac{1}{4}\%$ per annum for three months' deposits in sterling or, alternatively, $8\frac{3}{4}\%$ per annum for three months' deposits in Deutschmarks.

Comparing his two possible investment strategies for the three months' period then, he may do one of the following:

1. Place £1 on deposit and finish up with £1.0319.
2. Convert his pound into DM4.2650 and place the Deutschmarks on deposit for the period to finish up with DM4.3583.

Dividing each maturity amount by 1.0319, we now see that for every £1 he could have at maturity he could instead have DM4.3583/1.0319 = DM4.2236. This 4.2236 should be equal to the forward exchange rate.

If the reader is surprised by this, then he should consider how very much more surprising it would be if this were not the forward exchange rate. For in that case our investor would be able to sell his maturing marks at the true forward rate and make a profit versus option (1), or alternatively be able to sell his maturing sterling at the true forward rate and so make a profit versus option (2). The only rate at which neither route will provide a profit is 4.2236. Economic theory would suggest that such an arbitrage should never yield a profit and that the forward rate will indeed turn out to be 4.2236. But in practice this is seldom precisely true, although of course very nearly so, and there can be a profit for an arbitrageur.

This represents the most basic form of the classic cash/forwards arbitrage. We now move on to consider various methods of cross-market arbitrage which may be used as alternatives to, or developments of, this idea. As a first step we translate the idea to a more practical and real market level and look at the inverse of the above type of transaction, usually known to Forex and Eurocurrency dealers as 'interest arbitrage'.

Probably the simplest way to explain this idea is by way of a further example. Let us assume that a dealer is trying to determine whether he can 'produce' Deutschmarks to lend more cheaply by using the Eurodollar market and interest arbitrage, or by direct borrowing of Deutschmarks in the deposit market.

Data:

Spot DM/US$	2.3565
6 months' premium	370 points
6 months' Eurodollars	$9\frac{5}{16}$, $9\frac{3}{16}$
6-month period	182 days

Calculation if borrow US$ and convert to DM:

1. Borrow US$1 million at $9\frac{5}{16}$% for 182 days.
   Interest cost = US$47,080.
   US$ sum required at maturity = US$1,047,080.
2. Outright rate DM/US$ = 2.3565 − 0.0370 = 2.3195.
   To buy US$1,047,080 at 2.3195 will cost
   DM1,047,080 × 2.3195 = DM2,428,702.
   This sum of Deutschmarks will be required at the maturity date.
3. The sum of Deutschmarks that is available at the start date by conversion of the US$1 million at the spot rate is
   DM1,000,000 × 2.3565 = DM2,356,500.
4. The sum in Deutschmarks to be earned as interest over the six months is the difference between these two Deutschmark figures:
   DM2,428,702 − 2,356,500 = DM72,202.
5. Expressed as a rate of interest on the DM2,356,500 originally borrowed:
   $$72{,}202 \times \frac{360}{182} \times \frac{100}{2{,}356{,}500} = 6.0606\%$$

   This cost compares with the cost of borrowing the funds direct at the slightly higher market rate of 6.125%.

There are two key facts to note about the result of the calculation above. Firstly, the two answers of 6.060% and 6.125% are very close to one another. Secondly, they are not the same.

The reasons why they are very close to one another is not hard to seek. We saw above that forward exchange rates were derived from the difference between the interest rates of the two currencies involved. All we are doing

Arbitrage

now is running the calculation in reverse, calculating one interest rate given the other rate and the forward exchange rate. Logically, then, our two answers should be identical.

So why aren't they identical? The first reason why they don't line up exactly is because market prices are not static quantities; they are in continuous movement. A physicist will tell you that the surface of the Atlantic Ocean should logically be precisely horizontal, and indeed if the surface were static and without outside disturbance due to wind and tide, so it would be. The only way in which parts of the surface can be higher than other parts is if they are in motion at the time. Even then, every individual portion of the surface will be endeavouring to return to equilibrium, the totally flat condition of the physicist. In the absence of any outside disturbance this would eventually be achieved.

Market prices behave similarly, continually being pushed away from their equilibrium condition by new outside disturbances: buyers or sellers. The equilibrium level may be overshot for a period, or may itself be moved by one-way market pressure. The likelihood of everything being precisely at equilibrium at any given time is extremely small.

There are other, more technical reasons why the market may not act to arbitrage away small differences between direct and interest arbitrage rates, allowing an 'arbitrage turn' to persist.

As we have seen, a bank having dollar deposits but wishing to make Deutschmark loans has two routes open to it:

1. Lend the dollars to the market, and borrow the required Deutschmarks.
2. Convert the dollars to Deutschmarks and lend the funds as Deutschmarks.

Route (1) has some extra costs for a bank over route (2):

1. The dollar loan will use up part of bank X's credit line to whichever bank takes the dollars. This represents an opportunity cost in that the bank may now have to turn down other potentially profitable business with this bank over the months to come.
2. The Deutschmark borrowing will also use up part of the lending bank's credit line for bank X. This is also an opportunity cost in that the lending bank will be able to conduct less other business with bank X over the months to come.
3. Route (1) will increase the balance sheet by twice as much as route (2). This clearly affects balance sheet ratios including such aspects as liquidity ratios and capital adequacy ratios as well as management targets which may be defined in terms of return on total assets.
4. Both (1) and (2) involve transaction costs of dealing turns and possibly brokerage which will alter the relative attractiveness of the two routes as well as imposing a minimum cost for effecting the arbitrage.

For all the above reasons it is apparent that arbitrage turns will be created in the market, and that they are able to persist. On the other hand, if gaps become too big, it will become attractive to 'go round the triangle' and close the gap.

Arbitrage using paper

In the above calculation the dealer fixed the interest rate on the US dollar leg of the deal by simply borrowing the funds in the deposit market. This leg can alternatively be secured by reference to short-term paper yields such as the yield on certificates of deposit, floating rate notes, Euronotes, or bills.

If the interest rate for instance in the bill market is below the money market rate for the same currency and period then it will be attractive to replace the borrowing leg of the transaction with bill finance. This is the basis of the sterling bill arbitrage market in London, which may be used by companies to provide a very attractive form of finance for international trade transactions. The arrangement relies upon the fact that sterling bill rates for eligible bills in the London Discount Market are often significantly lower than inter-bank lending rates for sterling for the same periods. This favourable interest differential is not only available to a sterling borrower, but via the mechanism of interest arbitrage this differential can be translated into any other currency too, for instance, to produce US dollars or Deutschmarks at below the prevailing inter-bank lending rates for those currencies.

The reason that this differential is able to persist for appreciable lengths of time is that volume is restricted by the requirement for the bills to be 'eligible paper'. The principal requirements for eligibility are as follows:

1. Bills must identify the actual underlying import or export trade transaction being financed; eligible bills cannot be used for inland finance nor for the import of goods for the purpose of hire purchase or leasing.
2. The transaction must be shorter than six months and self liquidating.

Arbitrage using futures

There are a number of ways in which financial futures can be used as an alternative route to establish forward rates for currencies. Perhaps the simplest type of arbitrage is that between cash and futures for the forward rates themselves. Using actual market rates we have the following:

LIFFE dollar/sterling contract
Dec   1.4020
Mar   1.3965
Jun   1.3905

Forex market prices to these dates
Dec   1.4018
Mar   1.3960
Jun   1.3897

From this it is immediately apparent that prices as calculated from cash market rates were not identical to the prices at which the contracts were

Arbitrage

being traded on the exchange. To the extent that they are different there is scope for a profitable arbitrage between the cash and futures markets, buying in one market and selling in the other at a profit turn in the price. For example, in the situation above, the cash market forward exchange rate to March was 1.3960, while the futures market rate was 1.3965. Theoretically, and ignoring transaction costs, it would have been possible to buy forward sterling in the forward market and sell it on the futures market and make a riskless profit of 5 points.

More sophisticated arbitrage possibilities also exist on the London International Financial Futures Exchange (LIFFE) owing to the existence of three-months' interest rate contracts in both dollars and sterling. There are no less than four ways to arrive at a dollar/sterling exchange rate for a LIFFE settlement date:

1. Cash market forward rate.
2. Futures market forward rate.
3. Forward rate as calculated from the spot rate and a forward premium reckoned from the cash market dollar and sterling interest rates.
4. Forward rate as above, but with the premium calculated from the futures market implied interest rates for dollar and sterling.

Clearly, hybrids of (3) and (4) are also possible using cash for one leg and futures for the other.

Example

To illustrate the possibilities we will take representative rates from one trading day to calculate the results under cases (2) to (4) above for the June delivery date, which for simplicity we will assume to be identical to the six months' date.

Cash market
Spot dollar/sterling	1.6273
Six months' forward	1.6185
Six months' Eurodollar	$9\frac{5}{16}$
Six months' sterling	$10\frac{7}{16}$

Futures market
Dollar/sterling March	1.6235
Dollar/sterling June	1.6235
Eurodollar three months March	91.12
Sterling three months March	90.45

1. 1.6185 (given)
2. 1.6235 (from table)
3. Forward premium = $(10\frac{7}{16} - 9\frac{5}{16})/100 \times \frac{6}{12} \times 1.6273 = 0.0092$
   Outright price = $1.6273 - 0.0092 = 1.6181$
4. Equivalent three months' Eurodollar rate from March to June is $(100 - 91.12) + 0.25 = 9.13\%$
   Equivalent three months' sterling rate from March to June is $(100 - 90.45) + 0.25 = 9.80\%$

Forward premium March to June is given by
(9.80 − 9.13)/100 × $\frac{3}{12}$ × 1.6235 = 0.0027
Outright to March is 1.6235, so outright to June is
1.6235 − 0.0027 = 1.6208

The obvious differences between these four results represent arbitrage opportunities. Nor do the possibilities end there. The basic calculation is that the two interest rates and the forward exchange rate form a logical triangle; if you fix any two of them the third may be calculated. This is true of the three cash market entities, and also true of the three futures market entities. Any one cash market entity and one futures market entity enable us to calculate where the third should stand in both the cash and futures market. If they are not at exactly that level, then there is an arbitrage opportunity.

Some operators, using computer-based systems, can keep continuous check on these various arbitrage possibilities. Clearly this role is a minor one in the context of the market as a whole, but it does tend to ensure that futures market prices do not get too far out of line from the underlying cash market prices to which they relate. Arbitrage activity has the effect of increasing the depth of the market. A large order which the futures market could not perhaps otherwise absorb without a major price shift will tend to be taken out against the cash market by arbitrageurs.

All very useful, no doubt, when dealing in dollar/sterling, where there are futures contracts in both three months' interest rates, but what if the treasurer seeks to hedge against a shift in Deutschmark interest rates? Or Swedish kronor?

This too can be handled if we recall the foreign exchange swap relationship, approximately expressed as

Currency A forward premium per annum =
$\frac{\text{(Eurodollar rate − currency A rate)}}{\text{Spot exchange rate}}$

This formula is usually used from spot date; for example the forward premium between spot and the three months' date is used with the three months' Eurodollar rate to calculate the three months' interest rate for the currency concerned. But the same formula will also operate perfectly well for a future start date, and so can be used to derive 'futures prices' for any currency with an active forward foreign exchange market.

Eurodollar futures provide the Eurodollar input and the cash forward FX (foreign exchange) market provides the swap price (being the forward premium between the start date and finish date of the futures contract). This establishes a futures price for the currency concerned which may be used for hedging. The example which follows shows how.

Example
A company has a three-month rollover loan in French francs of $1 million equivalent. There are rumours that the currency may come under pressure in the near future (which does not help the treasurer as

his loan is financing a French franc asset) and the company seeks to hedge against any sudden rise in French franc rates that could arise as a result of the exchange rate pressure. His next rollover is nearly three months ahead, in March.

Rates:

	Dec	Mar
Spot FF/$	7.96	8.14
Three months' premium, points	900	1,750
Six months' premium, points	2,250	n/a
Three months' FF LIBOR	15	$18\frac{3}{8}$
March Eurodollar, LIFFE	89.96	90.14

Calculation:
Swap price, 3m to 6m = (2,250 − 900) = 1,350 points
Interest rate, premium over dollars:

$$\frac{1,350}{7.96} \times \frac{12}{3} \times \frac{1}{100} = 6.78\%$$

Implied futures rate for March Eurofrancs:
89.96 − 6.78 = 83.18 (i.e. 16.82%)

Action:
Sell 1 Dec Eurodollar contract at 89.96
Buy the swap at 1350 points in the forward FX market
The objective is to protect against any worsening of the existing 16.82% rate for the period concerned.

In March:
Swap price now is 1,750 points
Interest rate, premium over dollars:

$$\frac{1,750}{8.14} \times \frac{12}{3} \times \frac{1}{100} = 8.60\%$$

Implied futures rate for Eurofrancs:
90.14 − 8.60 = 81.54 (i.e. 18.46%)

Action:
Buy back the Eurodollar at 90.14
Sell the swap at 1,750 points

Results:
Loss on Eurodollar contract:
90.14 − 89.96 = 18 points × $25/point	= $ (450)
$ cost of swap 1,350 points at 7.96	= $(16,960)
$ proceeds from swap, 1,750 points at 8.14	= $ 21,499
Net gain on hedge	= $ 4,089
Increased cost of loan (18.375% − 16.82%)	= $ (3,888)
Hedge efficiency	= 105%

Notes
1. Although the actual three months rate from today as at the start of the hedge was 15% there is already nothing that can be done about the differential between this rate and the 16.82%, since the 16.82% is the rate today for the three months' period to commence in March.
2. Hedge efficiences can be greater or less than 100, according to whether they overshoot or undershoot. An efficiency of 105% is no 'better' than 95%, it is merely 5% off-target in the opposite direction.
3. The gain on the hedge could alternatively have been calculated as

   $(83.18 - 81.54) = 164$ points $\times$ \$25/point $= \$4,100$

   The \$11 difference is simply a rounding error. The version shown in the example has the merit of showing the sources of the various components of the gain.

It is of course possible to construct similar implied interest rate contracts with currency futures contracts. A straddle is the purchase of a future for one period offset by the sale of the same commodity for a different maturity. A currency futures straddle is equivalent to a foreign exchange forward premium as shown below:

	Futures	Forex
Sep	1.4931	1.4930
Dec	1.4955	1.4955
Mar	1.4980	1.4977
Straddle Sep/Dec	24 points	
Swap Sep/Dec		25 points

But:
1. Currency futures are only available in a few currencies.
2. Liquidity is poor.
3. Contract sizes do not correspond with the interest rate contracts, so that there are untidy 'loose ends'. For example the Deutschmark contract is DM125,000; if today's exchange rate is 2.6460 then we require 21.168 contracts to match one Eurodollar contract!

Forward Rate Agreements

Forward Rate Agreements (FRAs) came into use during 1984 as an alternative to interest rate futures. They were introduced by the London merchant banks as a new customer service designed to hedge interest rate risks in a simple manner. A particular demand for this type of instrument arose from the very many corporate borrowers who had facilities on a rollover basis with interest rates set at a fixed margin over some reference market rate such as the London Inter-Bank Offered Rate (LIBOR). Traditionally there had been little a company treasurer could do to protect the company from interest rate shifts that might occur between today and the next renewal date – perhaps a period of several months.

Arbitrage

Financial futures represent one theoretical solution, but in practice they are somewhat inflexible, and the margin and accounting problems associated with their use are cumbersome. The FRA, which is simply an agreement to fix a LIBOR interest rate for a future period, is much more flexible in use and avoids the margin and accounting problems encountered with financial futures.

The mechanics are as follows. The bank and the customer agree on the currency, amount, start date and period concerned. The bank then sets a rate for this period. For instance, suppose the customer wishes to hedge a Eurodollar loan rollover for a three-month period commencing 10 April, and the rate quoted is $9\frac{1}{2}\%$, and this rate is agreed between the parties. Nothing then happens until two business days prior to 10 April (that is, spot date), when the 'contract rate' of $9\frac{1}{2}\%$ is compared with the actual market LIBOR for the currency and period concerned, known as the 'settlement rate'. Any gain or loss resulting from the difference between the contract rate and the settlement rate is settled by a simple net cash payment on 10 April. If the settlement rate is higher than $9\frac{1}{2}\%$, a payment is due to the customer from the bank; if the settlement rate is lower than $9\frac{1}{2}\%$ a payment is due from the customer to the bank. The formula used to calculate the settlement payment is

$$\text{Settlement payment} = \frac{P(R-S)d}{100Y + Rd}$$

where

P = principal amount of loan
R = settlement rate, % per annum
S = contract rate, % per annum
d = number of days in period
Y = interest year, 365 days for sterling, 360 for dollars

In the early days of this market the banks wrote this type of contract for their customers and laid off the resultant risk in approximate slabs on the futures markets. Effectively the FRA was no more than a form of over-the-counter (OTC) or 'tailor-made' future. Later on, as the market grew, FRAs were traded between banks on the London inter-bank market as new instruments in their own right, and a market of considerable liquidity has been created in a remarkably brief period of time. Because this market tends to trade with different participants than the financial futures markets, and because of the difference in the nature of the instrument itself (in particular the fact that FRAs do not require either initial or variation margins) there is scope for FRA prices to drift out of line with those for the equivalent financial futures; in short, there is another interesting opportunity for cross-market arbitrage.

Nor of course is this limited to the most obvious possibility of the arbitrage between FRAs and futures; any of the various arbitrage possibilities discussed above when considering futures can also be undertaken by replacing the interest rate future leg with an FRA if that would work out cheaper at the time. And if working out your forward foreign exchange rates using FRA prices seems a strange way of going about it, then of course so it is – but if that should happen to be cheaper, then that is what cross-market arbitrage is all about.

Currency options

Nature of an option

A currency option provides the buyer with the right, but not the obligation, to exchange one specified currency for another at an agreed exchange rate (the 'strike price'). Normally this right may be exercised on any date up to and including a specified 'expiration date'. For this right the buyer pays the writer a premium at the outset; the writer is obliged to honour the contract to the buyer on demand. Clearly, it is in effect a form of foreign exchange insurance which protects the buyer from any downside risk should the exchange rate move beyond the agreed strike price, yet enables him to profit should the exchange rate move in his favour.

Derivation of premia

The essential difference between an option and a forward contract from the buyer's point of view may be summarised as follows:

1. He pays a premium.
2. He benefits from the 'upside'.

In both cases his downside is protected. So presumably the premium is the market's best estimate of the likely value of the upside. In turn the value of the upside, and thus the cost of the premium, will depend upon three main factors:

1. How long the option runs, i.e. how much time is available for the rate to change.
2. The recent level of volatility of the exchange rate in question.
3. How far the strike price is from the market rate now.

This last factor is usually expressed in the jargon as follows:

> If the exchange rate now is better than the strike price, the option is 'in-the-money'.
> If the exchange rate now is equal to the strike price, the option is 'at-the-money'.
> If the exchange rate now is worse than the strike price, the option is 'out-of-the-money'.

For instance, if the $/DM rate on a particular day was 2.6365, or, quoted in US or reciprocal terms, DM1 = US$0.3793, then on this date a Deutschmark call option with a strike price of US$0.40 would be 'out-of-the-money', while a Deutschmark call at US$0.36 would be 'in-the-money'. A typical set of three-month premia based on this spot rate of $0.3793 and a forward outright rate of $0.3853 might look similar to the example shown in Table 8.1.

Arbitrage

Table 8.1. Three months' premia, DM/US$.

Strike price US$/DM	Premia in points* Calls	Puts
0.3600	257	18
0.3800	118	69
0.4000	43	210
0.4200	12	410

* Points = 1/100 US cents
Spot = $0.3793
Three months' outright = $0.3853

At any given time there will be a choice of strike prices and expiration dates in the market and the premia will vary with these factors as follows:

1. The further maturity dates will have higher premia than the near ones.
2. For call options, the higher the strike price the lower the premium.
3. For put options, the lower the strike price the lower the premium.

The last two points are apparent from Table 8.1 and they introduce the concepts of 'intrinsic value' and 'time value':

1. The option premium may be thought of as the sum of the intrinsic value and the time value.
2. Intrinsic value is the profit that would arise if the option were exercised today.
3. Intrinsic value can never be negative, since at this level the option would not be exercised. (The buyer is under no obligation to exercise at a loss, and therefore presumably will not do so.)
4. Time value can never be negative, although it will fall continuously towards zero as expiration date approaches.
5. For either calls or puts, time value will tend to be at a maximum at the strike price closest to the current market exchange rate. This is because, in the case of an in-the-money option, as time goes by some of the existing unrealised profit could be lost; there is now a downside risk as well as an upside potential. Time value for in-the-money options will thus fall for options further into-the-money. Deeply in-the-money options may even have time values very close to zero.

All these effects are readily observable from the data shown in Table 8.2, where the original premia have been split into their intrinsic and time components.

Table 8.2. Three months' premia, DM/US$, with intrinsic and time components.

Strike price US$/DM	Premia in points Calls		Puts	
	Intrinsic	Time	Intrinsic	Time
0.3600	193	64	–	18
0.3800	–	118	7	62
0.4000	–	43	207	3
0.4200	–	12	407	3

Relationship to forward FX market

The levels of option premia are further constrained by the possibilities of arbitrage with the forward foreign exchange market. An outright forward foreign exchange contract would be represented on a conventional profit chart (where the vertical axis shows profit against a horizontal axis of exchange rate), by a diagonal straight line, rising from left to right. If the currency rises x% from the price dealt then proceeds will rise x% too; if the currency falls x% then proceeds will fall x%. So it behaves like buying a call on the upside, like selling a put on the downside. Indeed, buying a call and selling a put are together equivalent in effect to an outright forward purchase at the exercise price. This being the case, it would be expected that these two alternative routes would also be equivalent in cost.

The cost of the synthetic forward contract is made up from the call premium paid, C, less the put premium received, P, and the strike price or exercise price agreed, E. The cost of an outright forward contract to the same date is F. So we would expect that

$$F = E + (C - P), \text{ or}$$
$$(C - P) = (F - E)$$

This can be readily checked against actual market rates.

This has been done in the third rates table shown below (Table 8.3), using the same premia already used for three months' Deutschmarks.

Table 8.3. Call/Put differentials v. Forward market, points.

E Strike	C Call	P Put	C − P	F − E
3,600	257	18	239	253
3,800	118	69	49	53
4,000	43	210	(167)	(147)
4,200	12	410	(398)	(347)

Forward outright (F) = 3,853 points.

It is seen that the correspondence between the two columns for (C − P) and (F − E) is fairly good, while naturally it is not perfect. Clearly if the two columns were seriously out of line it would be possible to do arbitrage deals at a profit until the gap narrowed to that representing dealing costs. Several interesting consequences flow from this relationship:

1. The gap between call and put premia is fixed within a fairly narrow band by forward foreign exchange market prices.
2. If the outright price is equal to the exercise price then put and call premia should be roughly equal.
3. A lower limit for a call premium may be set as (F − E) and for a put premium (E − F); this arises by simple arithmetic since neither P nor C can be negative.

Arbitrage

4. For in-the-money options, since exercise can be made at any date and not just at the expiry date, the lower limit for call premia is more strictly defined as (F − E) or (S − E), whichever is the higher, where S is the spot price. For example, from Table 8.3, for 36 calls:

(S − E) = 3,793 − 3,600 = 193;   (F − E) = 253

(F − E) is therefore the higher and forms the lower limit to the call premium, which is actually at 257. Similarly, for puts the limit is (E − F) or (E − S), whichever is the higher. For 42 puts the figures are:

(E − F) = 347;   (E − S) = 407

The 407 thus forms the lower limit; actual put premium is 410.

5. A synthetic for any forward contract can be created from two option contracts.
6. A synthetic for any option contract can be created by a forward contract plus another option.

Fig. 8.1 shows the various possibilities for the creation of such synthetics.

Conversions and reversals

The correspondence between forward foreign exchange rates and option prices has been outlined above; conversions and reversals are transactions based on this equivalence which produce synthetic forward exchange contracts.

A synthetic forward bought contract is created by buying a call and selling a put. If this works out cheaper than the forward or futures market, then the synthetic bought contract, or synthetic long, can be matched at a profit by an offsetting sale in the forward or futures market. This combination deal is a conversion.

The equivalent arbitrage, creating a synthetic short by buying a put and selling a call, and then buying the offsetting forward or future, is a reversal.

For obvious reasons these types of transaction tend to be confined to professional market operators, but there is one by-product of the process which is of more general use to treasurers. Because conversion and reversal activity maintains price equivalence between the options, forwards, and futures markets it is possible to transform existing call options into puts or vice versa using the forward or futures markets. The relationships are

call option + forward sale = put option
put option + forward purchase = call option

Delta hedges

We have seen above that, at a given market exchange rate, the value of an option will vary according to its strike price. Conversely, the value of a given option will vary as the exchange rate moves. This variation is non-linear but may be treated as though it were linear when looking at the impact of small exchange rate shifts of the order of, say, 1%. Consider for example a

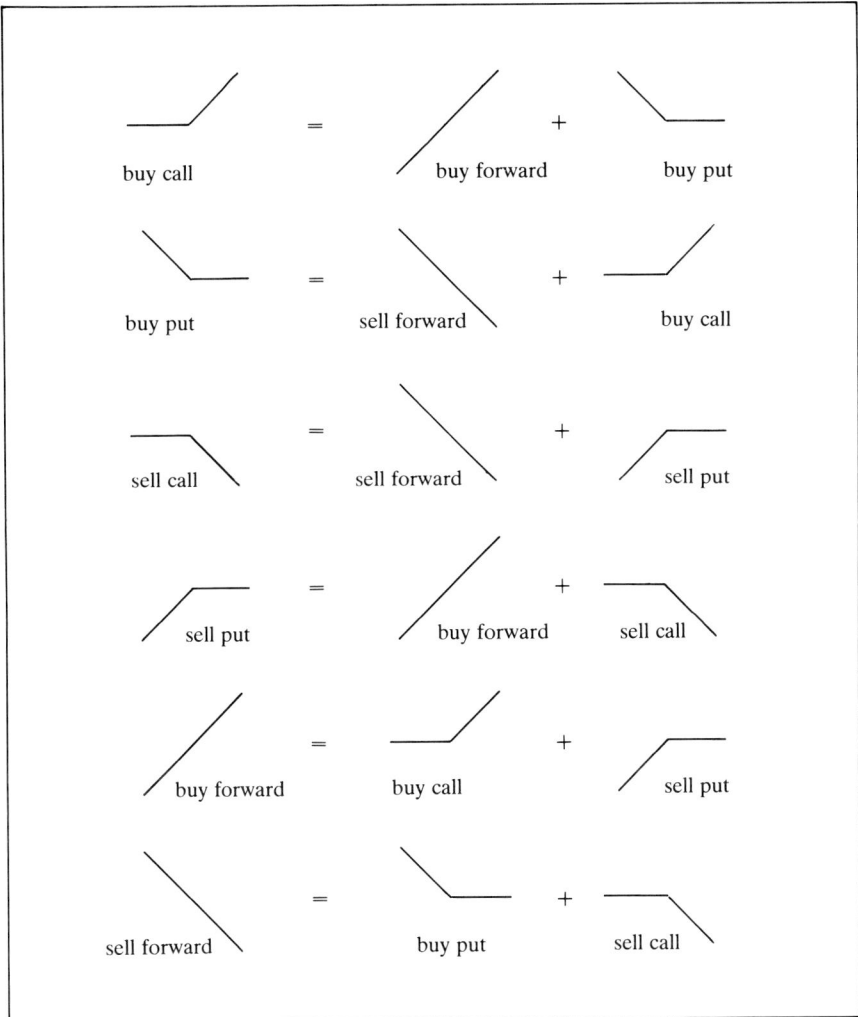

Fig. 8.1. Options/forwards relationships.

Deutschmark call option whose value might fall by $20,000 if the Deutschmark fell by 1%. It would be possible to hedge this position in an approximate manner by an outright sale of Deutschmarks against $2 million. The hedge is only approximate since although the value of the forward contract will change by $20,000 for every successive 1% shift in the rate, the same will not apply to the option, as each successive 1% move will result in a slightly different shift in the value of the option.

Nevertheless, the hedge is still effective to a useful extent; such hedges are known as 'delta hedges'. Delta hedges provide yet another arbitrage link between options and forward markets.

Interest Rate Guarantees

Following the growth of the market in foreign currency options, interest has grown in options on forward interest rates. This demand has been met by the development of the Interest Rate Guarantee (IRG).

An IRG can be used by either a lender or a borrower to obtain protection from an adverse shift in interest rates. A borrower's guarantee is taken when the buyer seeks compensation from rising rates; a lender's guarantee is taken when the buyer seeks compensation in the event of falling rates. An IRG provides the buyer with the right to receive an amount determined by the difference between LIBOR and an agreed contract rate as it exists for a given currency and period on an agreed forward date. The exercise of the option results only in a payment based on the difference between the two interest rates; no actual deposit transactions are involved (that is, net cash settlement only). The amount payable to the buyer on exercise is calculated according to the same formula as is used for FRA settlements (see page 130).

IRGs are thus similar in nature to FRAs with the obvious difference that the obligation to pay under the terms of the agreement (if rates move in favour of the buyer) rests solely with the guarantor, and should rates not move in favour of the buyer, the option may be abandoned. As with other types of option, the buyer pays a fee at the outset of the IRG. The effect of the transaction is that the buyer will obtain the eventual market rate, or the IRG contract rate, whichever is the more favourable to him; it has been aptly described as 'an option on an FRA'.

Following the introduction of IRGs by the banks, an inter-bank market rapidly grew up to trade the new instruments. Subsequently a number of exchange-based instruments have also been introduced by futures exchanges, usually offering an option on an existing traded interest rate futures contract. Again we see the growth of parallel, but not identical instruments, and the possibility of arbitrage. The main possibilities here are clearly to arbitrage IRGs against the equivalent exchange-traded instruments, and also to trade IRGs against FRAs or futures as a delta hedging arbitrage as described for currency options; and so back into the cash markets, and the Forex markets, and so on.

As time goes by and markets continue to proliferate, even more new instruments are bound to be developed. And as they do, even more parallel markets will be formed whose price relativities will tend to drift away from their equilibrium and create that precious little gap where the arbitrageur can make his living. If 'arbitrageur' as a word has a quaintly old-fashioned ring about it, there will be nothing old-fashioned about the new breed of cross-market arbitrageur operating in this complex environment. His world will be dominated by the quality of his computer systems. The systems will track the prices, identify the anomalies, possibly suggest appropriate courses of action, and keep control of the net position taken and the profit or loss accruing. But none of this will replace the qualities that have always been needed in the man who sets out to live by his wits as a cross-market arbitrageur; after all, no one ever set out into this specialised field because it was easy, but rather to respond to the challenge of the intricacies of cross-market arbitrage.

Index

acceptance of exchange risks, 14, 15–16
accounting
   and control, management, 25–27
   internal deals, 28–29
   issues in interest rates and currency swaps, 118–19
acquisitions, 43–45
American Depositary Receipts, 36, 39, 42–43, 45
American option, 91
arbitrage
   classical example, 35
   dangers in commodity trading, 54–55
   defined, 1–9
   inter-market, simple, 73–75
   opportunities in commodity trading, 52–54
   in practice, 100–102
   see also commodities; cross-market; currency; futures; interest; interest rates; securities

base currency, 90
bear put spread, 103
bogus arbitrage, 7
bull call spread, 102–103
buying option, 102–103

calendar spread, 105–106
cash, simple, against forwards arbitrage, 122–25
Certificates of Accrual on Treasury Securities, 43
Chicago Board Option Exchange (CBOE), 41, 101
Chicago Board of Trade (CBT), 58, 63
Chicago Mercantile Exchange (CME), 58
cocoa market, 52–54, 56
coffee market, 55–56

commodity trading in different currencies, 46–57
   arbitrage
      dangers, 54–55
      opportunities, 52–54
   currency risk coverage, 56–57
   futures trading, 47–48
   hedging, 55–56
   marketing, 49–50
   oil price shocks, 48–49
   soft commodity
      markets, 46–47
      pricing, 50–52
complex strategies on financial futures, 75–80
compounding interest arbitrage, 20–22
contango arbitrage, 5
contracts, financial futures, nature of, 62–64
control and accounting, management, 25–27
conversion, currency, 43
   options, 134
convertible bonds, 36, 37–38
corporate treasurer and swaps, 119–20
covered interest arbitrage, 16–20
covered option writing, 106
credit risk in swaps, 117
cross-market arbitrage, 122–36
   currency options, 131–35
   Forward Rate Agreements, 129–31, 136
   using futures, 125–29
   interest rate guarantees, 135–36
   using paper, 125
   simple cash against forwards arbitrage, 122–25
currency
   base, 90
   conversion, 43
   different *see* commodity trading futures, 63–64, 68, 69–70, 85, 87
   proxy and financial futures, 80–83

137

Index

currency *contd.*
  risk coverage in commodity trading, 56–57
  swaps, 114–15
    see also under interest rates
  see also options
customer needs marketing, 49–50

delta hedging, 134–35
demand market, 96
derivation of premia, 131–32
differential swaps, 115
dollar-pool investment, 34

Eurodollar futures prices, 66
European Currency Unit (ECU), 12, 30, 59
European option, 91
exchange delivery settlement price (EDSP), 61
exchange risks *see under* interest arbitrage
exercise price, 90
expiration date, 91
  time to, 96
external deals, 26–27, 28

financial evaluation of swaps, 115–17
financial futures *see* futures
fixed coupon securities
  long-term futures on, 63, 66–69
  medium-term futures on, 66–69
forward exchange cover, 24
forward/forward lending and borrowing rates, 64–65
forward prices, 51–52
Forward Rate Agreements (FRAs), 129–31, 136
forwards
  arbitrage, simple cash against, 122–25
  markets and currency options, 133–34
futures, 36, 58–87
  arbitrage using, 73–75, 125–29
  cash relationships, 64–70
  complex strategies, 75–80
  contracts available, 62–64
  currency, 63–64, 68, 69–70, 85, 87
  interest rates, 86
  markets, 58–60, 84–85
  practical considerations, 70–73
  simple intermarket arbitrage, 73–75
  synthetic instruments and proxy currencies, 80–83
  trading, 47–48, 60–61

Government National Mortgage Association (GNMA), 58
guarantees, interest rates, 135–36

hedging
  commodity trading and, 55–56
  delta, 134–35
  strategies and currency options, 102–107
  strategies and option trading, 106–107

interest arbitrage, 10–31
  comparisons, 12
  compounding, 20–22
  concept, 10–11
  covered, 16–20
  exchange risks
    longer term, 14–15
    possible acceptance of, 14
    problems of acceptance, 15–16
    uncovered, 12–14
  internal deals, 27–29
  management, 25–27
  open positions, 22–23
  swapping, 17, 23–25
  uncovered, 11–12
Interest Rate Guarantee (IRG), 136
interest rates, 97–98
  comparisons, 12
  currency swaps and, 108–21
    corporate treasurer and, 119–20
    credit risk in, 117
    financial evaluation of, 115–17
    legal, accounting and tax issues, 117–19
    market, development of, 109–13
    types of, 113–15
  futures, 86
    short-term, 62, 64–66
  guarantees, 135–36
  time value and, 97–98
intermarket arbitrage, simple, 73–75
internal accounting, 28–29
internal deals, 27–29
International Monetary Market (IMM), 58, 62, 63, 64, 73
International Swap Dealers Associations Incorporated, 117
intrinsic value and pricing, 95–96
investment, dollar-pool and sterling area, 34

legal issues in interest rates and currency swaps, 117–18
London Inter-Bank Offered Rate (LIBOR), 11, 113–14, 129–30, 136
London International Financial Futures Exchange (LIFFE), 58–59, 61, 62, 63, 64, 73–75, 77, 125–26
long-term
  exchange risks, 14–15
  fixed coupon securities, futures on, 63, 66–69

Index

management: control and accounting, 25–27
marketability, 50
marketing commodities, 49–50
market/s
  creation, 30
  currency options, profiles of, 91–95
  development, interest rates and currency swaps, 109–13
  financial futures, 58–60
  forwards, and currency options, 133–34
  futures, 84–85
  primary, 34–35
  profiles and currency options, 91–95
  soft commodities, 46–47
  supply and demand, 96
  see also cross-market
medium-term fixed coupon securities, futures on, 66–69
mirror-image, 27
models, pricing, 98–99
Modern Portfolio Theory, 42

new shares, 36, 38–41

obligations, 36
oil price shocks in 1970s, 48–49
open positions on interest arbitrage, 22–23
opportunity creation in securities arbitrage, 35–43
  American Depositary Receipts, 36, 39, 42–43, 45
  Certificates of Accrual on Treasury Securities, 43
  convertible bonds, 37–38
  new shares, issue of, 38–41
  options, 41–42
  stock futures, 42
  substitutable securities, 36–37
options, 41–42
options, currency, 88–107, 131–35
  arbitrage in practice, 100–102
  background, 88–90
  conversions and reversals, 134
  definition, 90
  delta hedges, 134–35
  derivation of premia, 131–32
  market, 36
    profiles, 91–95
  nature of, 131
  pricing, 95–98
    models, 98–99
  relationship to forward market, 133–34
  spreads, 103–105
  terminology, 90–91
  trading and hedging strategies, 102–107
over-the-counter (OTC), 100, 130

paper, arbitrage using, 125
Philadelphia Stock Exchange (PHLX), 101–102
practical considerations of financial futures, 70–73
premia, derivation of, 131–32
premium, 90
pricing
  currency options, 95–98
  models, 98–99
  oil shocks and, 48–49
  soft commodities, 50–52
primary markets, 34–35
producer needs marketing, 50
proxy currency and financial futures, 80–83
pure arbitrage, 7, 8

ratios/weighting and option trading, 105–106
reversals, currency options, 134
risks
  arbitrage, 43–45
  exchange *see under* interest arbitrage
'round robins', 29
  compounding, 20–21
  fully covered, 16–20

securities arbitrage, 32–45
  acquisitions, take-overs and risk arbitrage, 43–44
  classical arbitrage example, 35
  currency conversion, 43
  historical background, 32–34
  opportunity creation, 35–43
  primary markets, 34–35
  settlement, 45
securities, fixed coupon, futures on, 63, 66–69
seller of vertical spread, 104
selling options, 106
shares, new, 36, 38–41
short-term interest rates, futures, 62, 64–66
simple
  cash against forwards arbitrage, 122–25
  intermarket arbitrage, 73–75
Singapore International Monetary Exchange (SIMEX), 59, 62
soft commodities
  markets, 46–47
  pricing, 50–52
spot
  arbitrage, 5
  prices, 51
spreads, option, 103–105
sterling area investment, 34
stock futures, 42
strike price, 90, 96
substitutable securities, 36–37

139

Index

supply market, 96
swaps/swapping
  interest arbitrage and, 17, 23–25
  see also under interest rates
synthetic instruments, 80–83

take-overs, 43–45
tax issues in interest rates and currency swaps, 119
terminology, currency options, 90–91
time value and pricing, 96–98
trading
  financial futures, 60–61
  internal deals, 27–28
  strategies and currency options, 102–107

uncovered exchange risks, 12–14
uncovered interest arbitrage, 11–12
uncovered option writing, 106
underlying currency, 90

value and pricing
  intrinsic, 95–96
  time, 96–98
vertical spread, seller of, 104
volatility and time value, 97

wasting asset, option as, 97
weighting/ratios and option trading, 105–106